PREPARING BOYS FOR BATTLE

By Scott T. Brown

MERCHANT ADVENTURERS
Wake Forest, NC

Second Printing: March 2010

Merchant Adventurers, Inc.
220 South White St., Wake Forest, North Carolina 27587
www.scottbrownonline.com

ISBN - 0-9820567-8-8
ISBN - 978-0-9820567-8-3

Book Design by David Brown
Cover Design by Ryan Glick

Printed in the United States of America

DEDICATION:

We, Scott Thomas Brown and David Edward Brown dedicate this book to William Edward Brown, our wonderful father and grandfather. This book declares that sons should ask and fathers should tell of the great deeds of the past. Thank you Dad for your willingness to tell.

David and I are extremely grateful for Doug Phillips who fanned the flames of all things Iwo Jima. We reveled in her generational lessons at parades, celebrations, and filmings in Fredricksburg, Texas; the shooting of the film *League of Grateful Sons* in Hawaii, Guam, and on the top of Mt. Suribachi; and the many happy days our families spent together at multiple Memorial Day Celebrations in Wake Forest, North Carolina.

Thank you Arnold and Esther Pent for your input, encouragement, and investment through the years. Our time at your hideaway was enormously important in the conception and writing of this book. What happened there resulted not only in this book, but also the birthing of a vision that changed both our lives.

I also want to thank those who edited and contributed to this book through their labors of love. There were many friends and family members who rallied to help. Thank you to David's wife Monica and family members Mary Brown, Deborah Brown, Blair Brown, Claudia Brown, and Peter and Kelly Bradrick. Thank you friends, Dana Merrill, Stephen Sides, Ryan Glick, and Andrew Gillingham. We are particularly thankful for our heroes Bill Brown, Bill Henderson, Buck Bunn, Arthur Burry, and Eddie Bates.

Scott and David Brown

TABLE OF CONTENTS

HOW TO USE THIS BOOK

This is a handbook for dads to help them train their sons for battle.

In this book you will find lessons for manhood that arise from the WWII battle for Iwo Jima with its fighter planes, amphibious assaults, foxholes, cave warfare, and flamethrowers.

It contains seventeen critical exhortations that I believe fathers must deliver to their sons. Why? To discipline them to be the mighty warriors God intends them to be. These were the things I told my own son David as he was growing up.

This is a book about leading boys to be truly great boys—and someday, men. It uses a personal, modern example (the example of my father and some other men I've met) to illustrate what God has already said in Scripture.

It is appropriate to remember the WWII generation. That generation of warriors spent their youth laboring to eke out a living after the Depression. They forged their character on hard work and frugality. They were farm boys and clerks and ditch diggers. Most were not raised with silver spoons and almost none of them had much leisure time. Then they went to war and saved western civilization from the godless tyranny of Hirohito and Adolph Hitler.

A generation of heroes does not just pop up out of nowhere. It is prepared by its fathers.

Introduction:
THE BATTLEFIELD OF MY FATHER'S YOUTH

Perhaps no other individual battle is as well-known by the general populace as the battle for Iwo Jima. Some claim that the most famous picture in the history of photography was taken there of the men raising the flag on Mount Suribachi. This was the first foreign flag raised on Japanese soil in many generations, and it meant the death-knell to Japanese expansionism and ultimately, the end of the Pacific war.

Because Iwo Jima was the battlefield of my father's youth, it was also the vortex where everything in his family background was severely tested and revealed. William Edward Brown was a small-town boy, just 20 years old when he enlisted to fight for his country. He never could have imagined the ferocity of the battles he would face. Furthermore, he could not have anticipated the lasting impression these battles would leave—not only on his life, but on the life of his unborn children as well.

For many years I have thought of that island and what happened there. It was a world of foxholes, flamethrowers, unrelenting artillery blasts, bombings, jeeps, fighter planes, explosions, and death. Thousands of Marines were ushered into eternity while doing their duty. Many of my father's fellow pilots were lost until, one day, he found himself to be alone in his tent, the last one alive.

Alfred, Lord Tennyson said it well,

> Storm'd at with shot and shell,
> Bravely they rode and well,
> Into the Jaws of Death,
> Into the Mouth of Hell… [1]

My father was just a boy back then. They were all boys. It is shocking to think that it was nineteen- and twenty-year-old boys who flew B-29s and P-51 Mustangs and stormed the beaches. The youth of our nation fired howitzers and flamethrowers and dove on top of grenades. It was young people who saved the world from Hirohito and Hitler.

It was high-octane danger—and courage. Manhood was tested, forged, and tempered at Iwo Jima.

This is difficult to explain, but I love the island of Iwo Jima. For the men who were there, it was hell on earth, but for me it has been a rallying point for powerful principles of manhood.

Sixty years after the battle, in 2005, three generations of Browns returned to Iwo Jima and stood on the ground where the flag was raised on Mount Suribachi. It was thrilling for me to be there with my father and my son and daughter, to look over the battlefield and see with my own eyes the places my father told me about all my life. When I stood atop that mountain with my father and two of my children, it was one of the most beautiful places in the world to me. It is the land of my childhood dreams because it was the battlefield of my father's youth. This is where my father flew fighter planes, defended our country, and bought me a future.

I pray that the lessons he learned there and the stories he communicated to me will be multiplied for many generations.

THE BOOK I ALWAYS WANTED

This is the kind of book I always wanted to have as a young father, flashlight in hand, inside a tent reading to my children. I always wanted a book with three qualities:

> First, it had to bring the reader to the teaching of Scripture, which contains the secrets of "life and godliness" (2 Timothy 3:16). There is nothing more encouraging or practical or life changing than Scripture.

> Second, it had to be about real people and real situations in history, for I value history over fantasy.

> Third, it had to communicate facts that were interesting, exciting, and fulfilling to ponder.

Each chapter of the book you have in your hand contains all of the following elements:

A true story from the battle

Boys need to know history or they are lost in their own context. Most of the chapters begin with stories my father told me, something else I learned along the way from some of the men I have met, incidents from our trip to Iwo Jima, or stories from reading about the battle there. Near the beginning of many of the chapters you will find the words, "My father told me," because this is the emphasis of the book. I wanted to document the things he told me about his experience there.

Life application

Each story ends with some practical correlation to everyday life or an important concept to live by. Thus, I have taken the stories from Iwo Jima and looked to them for illustrations of something important for life today.

Scripture citations summarizing the life application

All of life must be seen through the lens of Scripture and then be governed by it. With these Scripture references, I am not saying that everyone saw it this way or that the people involved understood it the same I way I do. This is simply my own understanding of how to see the events through a Scriptural perspective.

My desire is that this book will reveal some of the historical aspects of the battle for Iwo Jima as seen through the eyes of men who were actually there. But more than that, I pray that my work in compiling the stories my father told me of the great deeds of God in his past might bear fruit in a particular way to equip boys to be courageous men – men ready for battle.

PREPARING BOYS FOR BATTLE

EVERY SON NEEDS TO HEAR
HIS FATHER SAY:
"Son, Don't Waste Your Youth"

And what more shall I say? For the time would fail me to tell of Gideon and Barak and Samson and Jephthah, also of David and Samuel and the prophets: who through faith subdued kingdoms, worked righteousness, obtained promises, stopped the mouths of lions, quenched the violence of fire, escaped the edge of the sword, out of weakness were made strong, became valiant in battle, turned to flight the armies of the aliens.

- Hebrews 11:32-34

CHAPTER 1
UNMATCHED BATTLE

On Iwo Jima the youth of a nation rose up to defend a homeland. They were just boys on that island—one side fighting on the surface and the other in tunnels below ground. How do you prepare a son in his youth for the battles ahead? How do you prepare your son for difficulties that he might face in the future? What follows are some ways that a father can come alongside his son so that he does not squander his youth.

Growing up and hearing about Iwo Jima from my father, I never realized the significance of that little island in the Pacific until later in life. In my youth, it was a place of boyhood dreams filled with foxholes and jeeps, P-51 Mustangs, and DUKWs (amphibious trucks), flak, explosions, and Japanese night attacks.

What I didn't realize as a boy was that Iwo Jima was one of the most unusual battlefields in the history of warfare. What happened there can never

be repeated. That five-week battle stands tall among the greatest battles in human history. Neither Napoleon at Waterloo nor George Washington at Yorktown saw anything like this. No comparison can be made to the Greeks battling at Marathon or Teddy Roosevelt and the Rough Riders storming San Juan Hill in the Spanish-American War.

Warfare will never see another Iwo Jima.

Contemplating Iwo Jima as a man, the question that keeps ringing in my ears is this:

How do you prepare sons for battles like this?

The Challenges

IMPREGNABLE FORTIFICATIONS.

Lieutenant General Holland M. Smith, the commanding general of the Fleet Marine Force in the Pacific said, "It was the most heavily fortified island in the world."[1] The tactical challenges were unmatched by any other battle.

There was no hope of surprise. The enemy had all the high ground, exposing our troops to every form of firepower. Every square yard of dirt was under Japanese crosshairs. Iwo Jima was a fight entirely on the enemy's terms.

On Iwo Jima, we had no advantages at any point in the battle from landing to leaving. There was simply nowhere to hide. We were on their carefully prepared turf. According to one observer, "They would have us caught between the high ground in the north and Suribachi on the south. They could plaster us from both flanks with mortars, artillery, and rocket launchers hidden in caves and pillboxes in the volcano and the northern ridges. They might even be able to keep us from reinforcing our first waves and then annihilate our forces already ashore."[2]

The terrain did not allow clear lines of battle. Never before had there been a battle with one side fighting on the surface of the ground and the other below ground. Imagine two great armies, the American forces maneuvering above and the Japanese below. 60,000 to 80,000 U.S. troops were on the surface or offshore while 23,000 Japanese were underground, criss-crossing battle lines through a complex matrix of tunnels and cave openings.

There were some sixteen miles of tunnels with three levels. The construction specification called for the tunnels to be built thirty-five feet below the surface to keep them unaffected by shelling. They were a minimum of thirty-three feet long, five feet wide and five feet high. These tunnels contained ammo dumps, field hospitals, running water, command posts, and, seventy-five feet down, the quarters of the lord of the underworld—General Kuribiyashi. The tunnels were designed with frequent turns of ninety degrees to provide cover from flamethrowers and other incursions. Connecting these tunnels were 1,500 rooms hewn into the rock. Everything was sunk in the

ground so that the enemy was not seen.

The Japanese fired from small holes in rock-camouflaged basements and thick blockhouses sunk into the earth. They had built 750 of these all over the island. They were composed of rounded reinforced concrete and were almost impregnable.[3]

How did they construct such a complex system? Korean slaves were brought to the island to dig the tunnels. When they were finished with the construction, most of them were executed.

UNREALIZED EXPECTATIONS

Even though we conducted the largest pre-invasion bombardment in the Pacific Theatre, the enemy was largely unaffected. We attempted to bomb the island into oblivion for seventy-two days, from December 8th to D-Day on February 19 ("D-Day" is the name given to the beginning of a planned attack, and should not be confused with the well-known "D-Day" at Normandy). Even so, the length of time was not enough in the opinion of the Marine generals. They wanted six months of pre-invasion bombardment, but Admiral Nimitz and President Roosevelt would only approve two months. This refusal embittered General Holland Smith and the others who would lead the charge on D-Day. "This will be the bloodiest fight in Marine Corps history," Smith said to Admiral Nimitz. "We'll catch seven kinds of hell on the beaches and that will be just the beginning."[4]

Unfortunately, the bombing did little practical good, although it did make many craters for our troops to jump in and out of when they came ashore.

This unrelenting bombardment did not subdue the enemy. A New York Times dispatch, written just after our troops landed, said this: "Iwo, a small island, has stood up under bombings and shellings as though it were fifty times its size. Time after time, after smashing attacks on Iwo, American planes would come back the next day to be greeted not only by anti-aircraft but by fighter planes in the air."[5]

UNRIVALED VIOLENCE

It is clear from all observers of the battle for Iwo Jima that the violence there was matchless among World War II battles. Time correspondent Robert Sherrod reported that Japenese and American dead at Iwo Jima had one thing in common: "They all died with the greatest possible violence. Nowhere in the Pacific War had I seen such badly mangled bodies. Many were cut squarely in half."[6]

Second Lieutenant Pete Zurlinden (Dayton, Ohio) wrote, "At Tarawa, Saipan and Tinian I saw Marines killed and wounded in a shocking manner, but I saw nothing like the ghastliness that hung over the Iwo beachhead. Nothing any of us had ever known could compare with the utter anguish, frustration and constant inner battle to maintain some semblance of sanity, clarity of mind and power of speech. As long as you could speak, you believed you had a slim chance to live. None of us would concede that death would have been a merciful coup de grâce. Everybody was seized with an insensate lust to live."[7]

On D-Day, there was a casualty every forty-five seconds, with almost 9,000 Marines on the beach in forty-five minutes. Throughout the battle we sustained 24,053 casualties, almost one Marine or corpsman becoming a casualty for every three who landed on Iwo Jima. These were the highest single-action losses in Marine Corps history. Of these, a total of 6,140 died.

"Almost one-third of all the marines killed in World War II were lost on Iwo Jima alone," states the Iwo Jima Survivors Association.[8]

The outfit that raised the flag on Mount Suribachi was actually destroyed from heavy casualties. When Easy Company cut across the 750-yard neck of the island and then started up Mount Suribachi, who would have thought the entire company would cease to exist by the end of the battle? Captain Dave Severence, E Company, 28th Marines described it in this way: "Easy Company started with 310 men. We suffered 75 percent casualties. Only fifty men boarded the ship after the battle. Seven officers went into battle with me. Only one—me—walked off Iwo."[9] Iwo Jima was an island of magnificent significance—and sacrifice.

It was a battle without rest.

It was the place where hundreds of men jumped on grenades to protect their friends.

It was where loyalty unto death was demonstrated over and over again.

Patrick Clancey writes,

> It is difficult to imagine any battlefield more closely resembling the biblical vision of Hell than the eight square miles of volcanic ash, pumice, and sand that even tanks, let alone Marines, could not easily move across—reeking of sulphur and brimstone, swept by bombs, bullets, and shellfire, and soaked in the blood of more than 26,000 dead. Truly the Prince of Darkness must have felt right at home.[10]

What does a father do to make sure his son is prepared for a battle of such great proportions?

Because fathers can never anticipate what kind of battlefields there will be in the future, they must prepare their sons for everything. Our boys need, deep within their hearts, the principles that they must be able to put into practice wherever they are at a moment's notice. They need the "whole counsel of God" planted early in their hearts so that they will know what to do in whatever state they find themselves. A father cannot afford to waste the youth of his son on things that will not fortify his mind and heart for the difficult or the evil day. Therefore a father should consider a lifestyle that allows him to say the same thing that Paul said as the spiritual father of the elders of the church in Ephesus on the beach at Miletus,

> For I have not shunned to declare to you the whole counsel of God. (Acts 20:27)

A Father Must

1. COMMUNICATE THE NATURE OF BATTLES AHEAD.

Fathers must have it in their minds that they are preparing their sons for specific battles they will face in the future. This is where the work begins, for a father ought to think through the particular challenges his son might face based on his knowledge of Scripture and his own experience. He needs to enumerate in detail what battles these might be. Every boy will grow up and face battles. It would be presumptuous to expect our sons to experience a trouble-free, battle-free life, so we must prepare them for conflict. Even though we know that the world is full of trouble, we secretly wish for a trouble-free life for our children. As responsible men, however, we know that every boy and every man and every family and every company and every nation will face battles over the course of their existences.

Youth is the time of preparation for those battles.

The book of Acts presents a picture of the types of conflicts that always go with the communication of the gospel. There are conflicts with pagan philosophers, religious authorities, and the government (Acts 17). This same pattern is seen over and over again in the book of Acts. These are the same general categories of conflict that a boy who is faithful to the message of Scripture will face. Here are a few questions you might ask yourselves:

> What are the theological/life issues my son will have to face?
>
> How will he defend creationism?
>
> How will he defend biblical gender roles?
>
> What false worldviews are there to dismantle?
>
> What are the defining issues of the day?
>
> How will he handle things when relationships are in crisis?
>
> How will he handle marriage and family situations?

How will he handle the pressures of the workplace?

How will he handle sins in his life?

The battle for Iwo Jima was incredibly fierce, and none of the boys who fought there ever could have dreamed they would face the kinds of terrors they experienced. To adequately prepare his son, a father must see to it that his son does not waste his youth. He does this by talking of the battles he has fought and working with his son to anticipate those battles yet to come. A father needs to recognize that it is the Lord who desires that sons be trained for battle. David said,

> Blessed be the Lord my Rock, Who trains my hands for war, and my fingers for battle—my lovingkindness and my fortress, my high tower and my deliverer, my shield and the One in whom I take refuge. (Psalm 144:1-2)

2. GIVE MEANINGFUL WORK AND WORK ALONGSIDE YOUR SON.

A father does this by making sure that his son has meaningful work to do every day. And what kind of work should it be? Productive work that contributes to the family economy. Real work that has tangible value in real life! Stretching work that increases his maturity! Challenging work that expands his skills! The days of youth ought to be a time of work experiences that prepare him for battle. And when the going gets tough and your son asks, "Why all this work?" a father can reply with confidence in his heart and vision in his eyes, "I am discipling you because I am preparing you to fight the battles that you will face some day." And "do not despise the training and admonition of the Lord" (Hebrews 12:5, Ephesians 6:1-4).

3. WALK BESIDE YOUR SON

If boys would become men, they would have to walk with men – not boys. One of the mistakes fathers make is sending sons off to be trained by someone else. It is the father's God-ordained responsibility to teach his children; particular harm comes from sending sons away in the early teen years when they are most needy of their fathers' instruction.

At the age when many sons are struggling most with authority and obedience to their parents, and when they most need their fathers' presence to secure that obedience, sons are often outsourced. This is the overwhelming family practice in Christendom today. This practice is, in part, socially acceptable because almost every church and institution removes teenagers from their parents in every program and meeting. Sometimes the separation happens because of difficulties between father and son, and removal seems easier than dealing with conflict. This option seems more attractive to a father when he considers himself inadequate to deal with problems, thus he transfers his responsibility for training his own son to others. Instead, he ought to be dealing comprehensively with the root problems and sins that are causing the conflict. Most of the time, fathers and sons are led apart by sin.

4. ILLUSTRATE FROM SCRIPTURE HOW IMPORTANT IT IS TO USE THE YEARS OF YOUTH FOR THE GLORY OF GOD.

The Bible is filled with examples of boys who not only did not waste their youth, but did great things.

- Josiah: The boy king who ushered revival into the land.
- Joshua: The young man who assisted Moses.
- Joseph: The boy who proved faithful amidst all adversity.
- Solomon: The boy who prioritized righteousness.
- David: The courageous boy who feared God more than man.

While David is most famous for killing the vile Philistine, Goliath, we must also remember that when he put that stone between the eyes of the giant, he was already an expert in music and poetry and the family business – as well as the art of slinging stones. His most important quality, however, was that he feared God more than man. While other men cowered, he rose up, fearing God alone. Whether he was under the stars as a shepherd or in the battlefield, he was about his father's business. David did not waste his youth.

These boys presented in Scripture did not waste the years of their youth, but instead rose up and served God in their generations. This is in sharp contrast to youth culture in our own day, where it is normal that thousands of youthful hours are given to games, entertainments, and fantasy. This kind of youthful diversion does not promote the glory of God.

In contrast to this youthful waste, there are many inspiring examples from history to the contrary. Some of the most significant exploits have been accomplished by young men. Charles Spurgeon was preaching at sixteen; Richard Baxter at twenty-three; John Calvin was a chaplain at age eleven and began preaching at twenty-two. The writers Shelley, Byron, and Keats, and the musicians Chopin and Mozart created some of their masterpieces when they were only in their teens. Even though some of these men may not have been godly, they exemplify the residing potential of youth. Also consider John Quincy Adams, who was a diplomat as a teenager, and David Farragut who commanded a captured ship at the age of twelve. Remember George Washington who wrote his Rules of Civility when he was only fourteen years old, and Jonathan Edwards who wrote his Resolutions when he was in his teens. These are just a few of the myriad existing examples of individuals who capitalized on the strength endued by God in their youth and did great things.

Additionally, there have been those who broadened that focus and captured the power of youthful endurance in mobilizing armies to accomplish their goals. In the ancient world, Alexander the Great took thousands of young men with him and conquered the ancient world by the time he was thirty. Hitler understood the power of a well-mobilized army of young people and created the infamous "Hitler Youth." The communists spend their communication resources on the young because they understand how important it is to tap into their passion and energy.

The testimony of the patterns of the best boys in Scripture indicates that youth should not be thrown away on inordinate game-playing and irrelevancies.

A Christian father is wise to help his son understand in every way possible how important it is to use his years of youth for preparation for great things—and great adversity. To do this, he needs to give his son great things to do. When he engages in great things, he will face roadblocks and problems that will test and toughen him. It is through the difficulties and trials of tasks of importance that he will be prepared for even greater exploits later on. And who knows, your son may end up in a battle that far exceeds the requirements of heart, soul, strength, and courage of an "Iwo Jima."

This is why fathers need to say to their sons, "Don't waste your youth." Then they need to come alongside them and help them to use their time in significant exploits.

5. TEACH HIS SON A BIBLICAL UNDERSTANDING OF TIME.

The first thing a father must do is ensure that his son does not waste the hours and the days and months of his youth. To impart this, he must have a sense of time and the prospect of wasting it that is consistent with the admonition, "Teach us to number our days that we may present a heart of wisdom" (Psalm 90:12). God is pleased to find us "Redeeming the time, because the days are evil" (Ephesians 5:16). This is critical since, "Every man's work shall be made manifest: for the day shall declare it, because it shall be revealed by fire; and the fire shall try every man's work of what sort it is" (1 Corinthians 3:13). "That he no longer should live the rest of his time in the flesh to the lusts of men, but to the will of God" (1 Peter 4:2). "He also that is slothful in his work is brother to him that is a great waster" (Proverbs 18:9).

These admonitions are not just for adults, for "Even a child is known by his doings, whether his work be pure, and whether it be right" (Proverbs 20:11).

Jonathan Edwards as a teenage boy developed seventy resolutions to guide him in the use of his time. Here is resolution Number Five:

> Resolved, never to lose one moment of time; but improve it the most profitable way I possibly can.

A father must have this same vision and understanding of time and see to it that his son does not waste his youth on trivialities. Fathers and sons must have the consciousness of time that is presented by David and his son Solomon.

> As for man, his days are like grass; As a flower of the field, so he flourishes. (Psalm 103:15)

> Man is like a breath; his days are like a passing shadow. (Psalm 144:4)

> Remember now your Creator in the days of your youth...before the silver cord is loosed, or the golden bowl is broken, or the pitcher shattered at the fountain, or the wheel broken at the well. Then the dust will return to the earth as it was, and the spirit will return to God who gave it. (Ecclesiastes 12:1-7)

Fathers and sons have a limited time together so they ought to redeem the time. They only have a finite number of days before the opportunity for personal training ceases. Robert E. Lee understood this principle and expressed it in a letter he wrote from the battlefield to his wife, asking her not to let his son waste his mind in frivolous reading.

Fathers, do not let your sons waste their youth.

"Son, Don't Waste Your Youth"

EVERY SON NEEDS TO HEAR
HIS FATHER SAY:
"Son, Lead Courageously"

"Now therefore, give me this mountain of which the Lord spoke in that day; for you heard in that day how the Anakim were there, and that the cities were great and fortified. It may be that the Lord will be with me, and I shall be able to drive them out as the Lord said." And Joshua blessed him, and gave Hebron to Caleb the son of Jephunneh as an inheritance.

- Joshua 14:12-13

Chapter 2
MOUNT SURIBACHI

Mount Suribachi. It was a fearsome objective that required a special kind of leadership to subdue. The duties of biblical manhood require this brand of leadership as well.

The duties of biblical manhood require decisive and courageous leadership, and it is a father's job to help his son develop these patterns in his boyhood. If the patterns are deeply impressed in boyhood, they will probably continue his whole life long (Proverbs 22:6). This is critical, for there will be many mountains to climb and much ground to secure for the kingdom of God.

There is something about a mountain that beckons us to conquer it. I have several towering mountain peaks etched in my memory: Mount Everest, Mount Fuji, Mount St. Helens, Mount Shasta, Mount McKinley, and Half Dome.

The most captivating mountain peak in my mind however, is not much of a mountain at all, but an inactive 556-foot-tall volcano the Japanese called Suribachi-yama. The Marines called it "Hot Rocks." It inspires a different kind of wonder than the signature mountain peaks of the world. Mount Suribachi represents an almost ominous kind of awe. And it reminds us of how important it is for boys to learn how to lead courageously.

Mount Suribachi has captured my attention since I was a little boy. Today it stands as a symbol of courageous, visionary leadership. It reminds me of how important it is to prepare boys to lead decisively. The Bible makes it clear that men are created to lead—for heavenly objectives. Not only that, but they are required by God to lead. God has vested in them the role of being the point man in strategic efforts.

Bill Henderson, who was part of the unit with the responsibility to conquer Suribachi, commented on the importance of taking personal initiative, "As a leader you've got to lead. You don't say, 'Boys, go take Hill 382,' you say, 'C'mon boys, let's take Hill 382.'"

The objective of Henderson's outfit was to cut the island in two at its narrow neck and then take Mt. Suribachi. That was the first major milestone toward victory.

One observer stated, "Suribachi seemed to take on a life of its own, to be watching these men, looming over them....The mountain represented to these Marines a thing more evil than the Japanese."[1] It needed to be taken from the enemy. But to get it the gates of hell would have to be stormed. Many would die before we would raise our banner on that mountain.

I am confident that the United States Marines had the same thought in their minds that Caleb had in his when he said, "Give me this mountain."

Young men need to be trained to think like Caleb. He knew that the dominion of the Lord was the only reasonable answer to the evils around him.

This rock fortress called 2,000 Japanese soldiers Atsuchi, who operated officers. General Kuribi- to last a week or two. He  Suribachi was manned by more than under the direction of Colonel Kanehiko somewhat independently from other yashi figured that these 2,000 might be able misjudged. The 28th Marines quickly defeated the Japanese strongholds as they pushed across the island's neck and, on D+1, hit the mountain. During the assault, Colonel Atsuchi was killed by 75 mm tank fire as he looked out the entrance of his cave. In spite of this loss, his soldiers fought on from what would become their burial caves. This complex natural fortress was further outfitted with over one hundred thick-walled bunkers, or blockhouses, which were connected by dozens of rock caves. It has been rightly called a "honeycombed killing machine." Though the cave openings were camouflaged, they could be seen when firepower began pouring out of them. My dad said there was so much enemy firepower coming from the fortress that it lit up like a pulsating Christmas tree.

Mount Suribachi provided the Japanese with an effective vantage point; almost any target on the island was visible from the top. This was one reason the first day of battle was particularly bloody. Anyone could be picked off wherever he was on the island. There was one Marine casualty for every yard gained on D-Day, February 19, 1945.

Elsewhere, the morning light on D+1 revealed the discouraging sights of the chaos created along the beaches by the combination of Iwo Jima's wicked surf and Kuribayashi's unrelenting barrages. In the words of one dismayed observer:

> "The wreckage was indescribable. For two miles the debris was so thick that there were only a few places where landing craft could still get in. The wrecked hulls of scores of landing boats testified to the price we had to pay to put our troops ashore. Tanks and half-tracks lay crippled where they had bogged down in the coarse sand.

Amphibian tractors, victims of mines and well-aimed shells, lay flopped on their backs. Cranes, brought ashore to unload cargo, tilted at insane angles, and bulldozers were smashed in their own roadways."[2]

With the mountain looming overhead, the Marines prepared their assault:

The 28th Marines had suffered nearly 400 casualties in cutting across the neck of the island on D-Day. On D+1, in a cold rain, they prepared to assault the mountain. Some of the 105 mm batteries of the 13th Marines opened up in support, firing directly overhead. Gun crews fired from positions hastily dug in the black sand directly next to the 28th Marines' command post. Regimental Executive Officer Lieutenant Colonel Robert H. Williams watched the cannoneers fire at Suribachi "eight hundred yards away over open sights."[3]

The Marines were totally exposed to the Mount Suribachi positions, and there would be no victory without its fall. It did fall. When that happened and our flag was raised, witnesses say that you could hear the whoops and the hollers and the cheers rise up from all over the island.

It was on this volcano that one of the most famous pictures in history was taken by Joe Rosenthal. This moment was bigger than life for the Japanese. For the first time in 5,000 years, a foreign flag flew on Japanese soil.

For the United States Marine Corps, Mount Suribachi was like the devil himself. It had to be taken, or there would be no winning of the Pacific War. If we could not take Suribachi, the Japanese would continue their expansionism. It was a key strategic target.

But, the moment after it was taken, the mountain became their own and was transformed. Communications equipment and observation posts were set up to monitor activity on the island, and what was once a horrible threat became a comfortable asset.

My dad stood on that mountain not many days after the flag was raised. He and his friend Arthur Burry jumped in an unmanned jeep one day

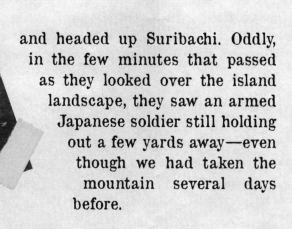

and headed up Suribachi. Oddly, in the few minutes that passed as they looked over the island landscape, they saw an armed Japanese soldier still holding out a few yards away—even though we had taken the mountain several days before.

For as long as I can remember, I have pictured my dad standing there, looking down through the smoke and dust at the wreckage of mangled metal and wrecked vehicles and sunk vessels clogging the beach. Since I was a boy, I have replayed that scene in my mind a million times as if I was there.

When the enemy was cleared from Mount Suribachi, it became a symbol of safety for the pilots seeking a friendly runway. For the flyboys, it meant "Home Sweet Home." It brought sighs of relief after many dangerous missions. When my dad was coming in from a raid, Suribachi was a refreshing sight. It was like an angel in the Pacific Ocean beckoning him home, saying, "Everything is okay now – you're home."

This transformation was the direct result of courageous, visionary leadership. Here are a few items to consider for preparing a visionary son who has it in him to "take that mountain"—whatever it might be.

A Father Must

1. LEAD COURAGEOUSLY FOR TRANSFORMATION AND TEACH HIS SON TO DO THE SAME.

Like the transformation of Mount Suribachi, when courageous vision is employed, something horrible can be transformed into something wonderful. The mountain symbolizes how things ruined by evil can be restored. Isaiah prophesied of this,

> Those from among you shall build the old waste places; You shall raise up the foundations of many generations; And you shall be called the Repairer of the Breach, The Restorer of Streets to Dwell In. (Isaiah 58:12)

Our boys on Iwo Jima set themselves to routing the enemy from that rock fortress, and now it belonged to them. They overcame the gates of hell. Suribachi, as evil as it was under enemy control, became an Ebenezer—a physical reminder of the deliverance God had accomplished. This is the job of manhood: an objective is identified, the plan is crafted, and an effort is mounted toward achieving it—no matter the cost.

Sons need the maturity to see the things that have been ruined by evil, and instead of cowering back, to press forward with Christ and His kingdom. One of the principles of maturity and spiritual wisdom that fathers need to pass on to their sons is that nothing is too far gone. Because God is mighty to reclaim ruined territory, we should never give up in the dark day, but persevere as we reclaim the waste places.

2. RECOGNIZE THAT MEN LEAD IN MULTIPLE WAYS.

There are several elements of God's requirements for men in leadership. First, God gives them the leadership of their own lives. We might call this self-government. In this realm, a boy must master his affections, activities, thoughts and meditations of his heart. To accomplish this he must have particular goals and objectives. Second, he must be prepared to provide leadership in other realms. For example, a son will most likely be called upon to provide leadership for a wife and children. Third, God may give him leadership of companies or even of nations. Each of these particular challenges of manhood has its own strategic objectives which must be discharged.

3. KNOW THAT BIBLICAL VISION IS THE STARTING POINT.

Men are designed by God to perform the function of visionary leadership, but ours is a derivative leadership. We are only authorized to draw from the mind and heart of God in all of our leading. The Bible teaches us God's will – His mind and heart – so we must teach our sons this is where all vision should begin. Scripture paints a picture of life and relationships, church and home, work and government that is the only reliable pattern for our lives as visionaries. We ought to conform our visions to the Word of God (Romans 12:1). Boys must understand early in life that "Without vision the people perish" and that it is only a biblical vision that will profit.

As we train our sons how to be visionary leaders, we must be certain they do not lead without the right reference point. They must lead under the authority of their Lord—the Lord Jesus Christ. If they create their own visions they will most likely only produce wood, hay, and stubble. The apostle Paul said it this way, "But I want you to know that the head of every man is Christ, the head of woman is man, and the head of Christ is God" (1 Corinthians 11:1-16).

They must have vision, but they must be sure that it is a biblical vision.

4. TEACH THAT A BOY'S VISION SHOULD BE CONSISTENT WITH HIS CALLING.

Each man's goals should be consistent with his particular calling. Men have different gifts and require the wisdom of God to determine what things He has created them to accomplish.

> Who then is Paul, and who is Apollos, but ministers through whom you believed, as the Lord gave to each one? I planted, Apollos watered, but God gave the increase. So then neither he who plants is anything, nor he who waters, but God who gives the increase. Now he who plants and he who waters are one, and each one will receive his own reward according to his own labor. For we are God's fellow workers; you are God's field, you are God's building. According to the grace of God which

was given to me, as a wise master builder I have laid the foundation, and another builds on it. But let each one take heed how he builds on it.

For no other foundation can anyone lay than that which is laid, which is Jesus Christ. Now if anyone builds on this foundation with gold, silver, precious stones, wood, hay, straw, each one's work will become clear; for the Day will declare it, because it will be revealed by fire; and the fire will test each one's work, of what sort it is. If anyone's work which he has built on it endures, he will receive a reward. If anyone's work is burned, he will suffer loss; but he himself will be saved, yet so as through fire. (1 Corinthians 3:5-15)

5. EXPRESS THE LEVERAGE OF DECISIVENESS AND PERSEVERANCE IN LEADERSHIP.

Clear objectives, courage and endurance are always required for godly leadership. There must be a jump-off point when specific objectives are engaged. Caleb was expressing this decision when he said, "Give me that mountain" (Joshua 14). Often men sit idle for years when they ought to be moving forward. Caleb's fortress-taking faith, was not a passive faith, but moved out with vigorous action. His action was completely under the authority of God. Six times in the chapter we are told that Caleb "followed the Lord." He was full of the Lord, and he was decisive.

In the book of Joshua, we see dedication to the end. This obedient vision was exemplified when Joshua comprehensively committed to the charge God had given him in the battle for Ai. "For Joshua did not draw back his hand, with which he stretched out the spear, until he had utterly destroyed all the inhabitants of Ai" (Joshua 8:26).

The boys who attacked Iwo Jima and vanquished Mount Suribachi are a good example of what it means to see an objective, accept the challenge, and endure the suffering. They accommodated themselves in willingness to do the will of their superiors. This is how courageous leaders operate, they see what needs to be done, and then take action and finish the job.

6. SHOW THE POWER OF VISION.

The leaders of the battle for Iwo Jima clearly understood this and saw Suribachi as a part of the vision. They went through trouble to get it, because they understood how important it was to the larger picture.

Vision was the only reason the fighter pilots were brought to Iwo in the first place. It was an act of faith. What was my dad, the fighter pilot, doing on a ship heading toward Iwo Jima? There were no planes on Iwo to fly, and there were still 22,000 Japanese soldiers dug underground in a vast matrix of tunnels honeycombing the island holding a vow, each one, to kill ten Americans before they died. Iwo was only a tiny rock in the hands of our enemies. But for the American generals, the island was already taken—at least in their minds. And because of their vision, on paper, they were turning Iwo into an air assault station to destroy Japan. They had squadrons of pilots, runway material, and hundreds of airplanes on the way as if they had already taken the island. So there was my father, a fighter pilot, heading to an island with no planes and no air base. He was fulfilling the vision.

This is what courageous leadership is all about. You see in your mind's eye what you are charged to do and then you set your course. And you may do things that seem to others like risk and comprimise. But you see completion. Our sons need to know how to craft a godly vision, and then spare no effort to achieve it.

7. KNOW THE IMPORTANCE OF SMALL THINGS.

Often the little things have a big impact for good or evil depending on who governs them. Iwo Jima was a little island only two and a half miles wide and five and a half miles long, in the midst of a vast ocean, yet it had a big impact.

Tim Challies, recognizing the significance of this little island, writes,

"There are many lessons we can learn from the Pacific Campaign. Some apply to warfare, but others apply far beyond. One of the most important is this: little things lead to big things. This is as true in warfare as it is in the hearts of men and women."[4]

He quotes Horatius Bonar who wrote,

"The avoidance of little evils, little sins, little inconsistencies, little weaknesses, little follies, little indiscretions and imprudences, little foibles, little indulgences of self and of the flesh, little acts of indolence or indecision or slovenliness or cowardice, little equivocations or aberrations from high integrity, little touches of shabbiness and meanness, little indifferences to the feelings or wishes of others, little outbreaks of temper, or crossness, or selfishness, or vanity--the avoidance of such little things as these goes far to make up at least the negative beauty of a holy life."[5]

There are no little islands, attitudes, actions, or sins. One small thing leads to another and another, and sometimes they become so large they overtake us. This is why we have to be very careful with what we involve ourselves. Even small things represent a direction we are going.

In the plan of God, every boy will someday be a leader; a good one or a poor one. He may someday, effectively or ineffectively, lead a family, a business, and a church. Maybe even a country at war.

But in all things, small or great, a boy needs to hear his father say, "Son, lead courageously." In so doing, a father will help his son be able to hold his head up, look at the looming shadow of Suribachi and say, "Give me that mountain!"

"Son, Lead Courageously"

EVERY SON NEEDS TO HEAR
HIS FATHER SAY:
"Son, This World is Not Your Home"

Let not your heart be troubled; you believe in God, believe also in Me. In My Father's house are many mansions; if it were not so, I would have told you. I go to prepare a place for you. And if I go and prepare a place for you, I will come again and receive you to Myself; that where I am, there you may be also.

- John 14:1-3

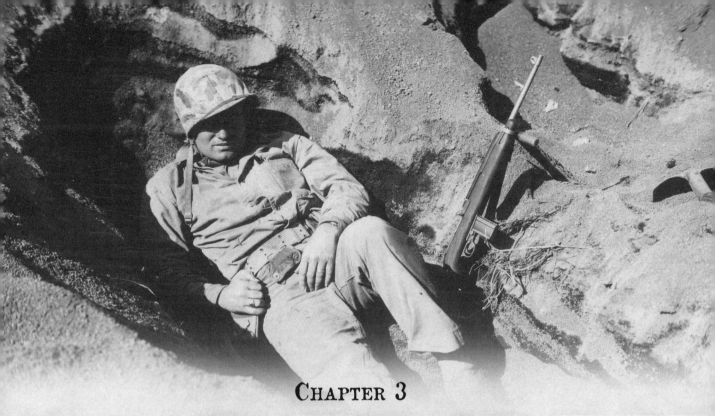

CHAPTER 3

LIFE IN A FOXHOLE

Every boy loves a foxhole. When I was a boy, my dad made me the proud owner of an army surplus folding shovel and a large Marine Ka-Bar knife that he brought back from Iwo Jima. These two items brought to life the stories he told me about his experience in the foxholes on Iwo Jima.

My mother reminds me that I was always digging my own foxholes all over our back yard and on the beaches in Southern California with that shovel and knife. She says that one time she was concerned because I excavated under the foundation of our house a bit too far. Back then, when I was six, I knew all about foxholes because my dad told me he dug one on Iwo Jima. I had such an innocent, boyish understanding of foxholes.

My dad spent two weeks living in foxholes on Iwo Jima. His experience taught me that a foxhole sums up the privations and exposures of war:

- Lack of protection from enemies
- The reality of death right next to you
- Lack of shelter from the elements
- The temporal nature of your position
- Lack of cleanliness and susceptibility to sickness
- Horrors of surprise in the night
- Mind-numbing sleeplessness
- Lack of rest from danger

There were nightly insecticide showers as planes sprayed DDT over the whole island to kill vermin like flies, mosquitoes, and maggots. In a foxhole, my dad was totally exposed to what fell from the sky. He was not in control of his environment.

It was an island of smoke, dust, and ash. The air he breathed was always heavy-laden with acrid smoke from explosives and burning metal, rubber, and foliage. There was so much bombing and shooting and driving that

dust was always falling, blanketing everything and filling the air. Dust was stirred up from airplanes landing, moving trucks, advancing tanks, and explosions; the soldiers were covered with it and choking from it.

Foxholes were not the healthiest places. Dad was in a foxhole for ten days until the flight surgeons ordered that the Army Air Corps pilots be put into tents because of excessive sickness. The Marines remained, hunkered in the slim protection of their holes.

There was a reason the Japanese called Iwo Jima "Sulphur Island." The volcanic activity caused a stinking, rotten egg smell. Foxhole diggers found hot rocks and hot water springs below the surface as they dug. The code name for my dad's combat mission was "Hot Rocks." Some of the foxholes were not only assaulted from above by showers of insect poison, dust and stench, but were hot, muggy, wet, and stinking of sulphur from the very island below.

There was the deafening 24/7 auditory reminder that the enemy had not yet been dislodged. One hundred feet from my father's foxhole was a battery (a dozen) of 105 mm howitzer guns that fired all night and all day, targeting Japanese positions on the island. Goodbye, sleep.

During these wakeful times, the night-time view from a foxhole was eerie. Not only was there the constant deafening sound of artillery, bombs, and gunfire, but the night sky was always filled with strobe-like flashes from artillery and the bright overhead illumination of exploded star shells which were launched to give our troops visibility of enemy movements on the ground.

One of the biggest problems with foxholes on Iwo Jima was that they were shallow and unstable. The worst places were on the assault beaches where it was like digging in oatmeal. The sand ran back into the hole as fast as the men tried to take it out.

When I visited Iwo Jima with my father during the 60th anniversary of the battle, I was amazed at how exposed his foxhole location was to enemy artillery fire. He was right out in the open. It was striking to see with my own eyes the looming form of Mount Suribachi and know that, with the right kind of firepower, the enemy could hit almost any position on the island – foxholes or not.

What happens in a foxhole is a jarring wake-up call. Though small, a lot happens there. It gives a dramatic illustration that this world is not our home. A foxhole is a microcosm of life, but with all of the difficulties of life experienced in their most concentrated and extreme forms. The discomforts and threats one experiences in a foxhole foreshadow many of the trials men face in life.

Those trials should drive most men to their knees.

Foxholes epitomize the insecurity, the danger, the exposure, the filth, the death, and the stench of war. They make a dramatic statement to all who live in them that this world is transitory, that life is a vapor. These reminders often make men face their mortality. And, of course, it is from here the term "foxhole conversion" comes. The realities of the frailties of life and the extreme danger cause men to remember their Maker and some are truly converted. Others, however, leave their faith behind when they move to more comfortable accommodations.

The things our boys faced in the foxholes of Iwo Jima are the same kinds of things our boys will face in life.

A Father Must

1. PREPARE HIS SON TO RIGHTLY RELATE TO EARTHLY COMFORTS AND ACCOMMODATIONS.

A father's training can mean the difference between a boy's falling in love with this world (and everything it has to offer in entertainment and comfort) or falling in love with heaven. It's a high stakes business. A father, by his own priorities and instruction can assist his son in forgetting about heaven and thinking only on the comforts (or discomforts) of his ride in this life. He can either sharpen or dull the awareness of important things.

2. LEAD BY EXAMPLE.

Training a son begins with a father's behavior, which is always a genuine expression of his heart. This means he has a lifestyle and a vision that will guide his son into a proper understanding of earthly and heavenly things. If your desires for earthly accommodations are too great, your son may become like you. Your son may gain the whole world and lose his own soul by following your example.

If a father is troubled and whines about his accommodations, or degrades other people's accommodations, he may find that he has raised an unthankful son who is dissatisfied with the provisions of God. A father's dissatisfaction can stimulate a son's dissatisfaction with his accommodations and might even turn him into a whiner. The antidote for this is a heart-level knowledge of God's provision. Jesus spoke tenderly to his troubled disciples about this problem,

Let not your heart be troubled; you believe in God, believe also in Me. In My Father's house are many mansions (John 14:1-3).

3. RECOGNIZE THE INADEQUACIES OF EARTHLY DWELLINGS.

The confrontations of life in a foxhole warn us about these frail earthly dwellings we now inhabit. As we move among various accommodations in this life, no matter how rugged or plush they might be, we must face the reality that all earthly homes are inadequate. What matters is the spiritual condition of the inhabitants. What matters is that they complete the mission to which God has called them.

Think of Abraham, who left Ur and did not know where he was going. He never had a house, just a tent. The only land he owned was a gravesite for his wife. Yet this didn't seem to bother him because he was looking for a city made without hands. He was fulfilling the mission to which God called him. The accommodations were secondary. Contrast this with the desire in our hearts to seek every comfort and amenity.

Because of the frailties of earthly dwellings, fathers should instruct sons about the adequacy of heaven alone. This home is only a temporary foxhole and can be broken into or destroyed at a moment's notice. Sons need to clearly understand that because our dwelling places here are temporary, their purpose is not to fulfill all their dreams.

4. SHOW THE RELATIVE IMPORTANCE OF MISSION AND ACCOMMODATION.

As we train our sons, our first objective ought to be to help them understand the greatness of their mission and insignificance of their accommodations. Boys need to understand that accommodations do not have to limit their goals. Life will not always go as planned, sometimes it will be hard. Boys need to understand this from the beginning through a father's instruction.

Even the most well appointed homes are always temporary and are nothing compared to the heavenly dwelling places God has prepared for His people. For this reason, it is silly for us to fall in love with those earthly dwellings – even though they might be much better than battlefield foxholes. Hebrews 11:16 shows a more reasonable way,

> But now they desire a better, that is, a heavenly country. Therefore God is not ashamed to be called their God, for He has prepared a city for them.

5. UNDERSTAND THAT SHALLOW MEN AND BOYS FALL APART.

Collapsing under the pressure of loss is not a manly quality. We don't want our boys to be so shallow that they fall apart if they lose their earthly dwellings. We need to get boys ready for action when they lose their homes or their jobs or whatever possessions they might have. They will be tempted to fall into despair, but we must help them to be ready with positive "knee-jerk" reactions. For example, if his home falls down, burns down, blows up, floods or rots, he needs the mental preparation that activates him to just dig another "foxhole." Earthly dwellings provide no security or protection. Only God can provide that. Train up sons who are strong in spirit, who are capable of happily getting to work when disaster strikes—digging the next foxhole.

6. VALUE ASSETS THAT ARE TRUE ASSETS.

Because your homes are temporary, help your son to know that his greatest assets are spiritual assets. How tragic it is when a young man is held back by his possessions, like the rich young ruler, who "was sad [at the words of Jesus] and went away sorrowful, for he had great possessions" (Mark 10:22). I have met many men who seem to have an obsession about giving land to their children. Please don't misunderstand me here, for I think it is a good and godly thing to give a house or land to your children. Proverbs 13:22 does say, "A good man leaveth an inheritance to his children's children," but I do not want my son to overvalue his house or his lands to the degree that he would be tied to them in any way or feel obligated to them if God called him to other things. Often men do not go where the Lord has called them because they have overvalued family land and held tightly to it, making it a worldly tether on their ankle, often resulting in compromise.

It is not the outward appearances or worldly possessions that matter, for they can be swept away in a moment. It is the inner spiritual resources that are the treasures of the kingdom of heaven. When these are cultivated, there is strength for anything life might present.

It doesn't matter so much where a man lives, but what lives inside the man.

Spending time in a foxhole on Iwo Jima helped many of our boys understand the frailties of the accommodations in this life. May we all see our everyday foxholes and remember the Christian's true home is elsewhere.

In a foxhole, there is a lack of protection from enemies. In life, you will not always be perfectly protected from our enemies

This world is not your home.

In a foxhole, there is the reality of death right next to you. In reality, a long life is not promised to any.

> This world is not your home.

In a foxhole, there is a lack of shelter from the elements. In life, there may be seasons of wandering and homelessness.

> This world is not your home.

In a foxhole, your position is temporary. In life, don't put your hope in temporary things.

> This world is not your home.

In a foxhole, there is a lack of cleanliness and susceptibility to sickness. In life, sickness often comes to the righteous.

> This world is not your home.

In a foxhole, there are the horrors of surprise in the night. In life, there are surprises in the night.

> This world is not your home.

In a foxhole, there is mind-numbing sleeplessness. In life, there will be wearisome sleeplessness.

> This world is not your home.

In a foxhole, there is a lack of rest from danger. In life, we are promised "in this world you will have tribulation."

> This world is not your home.

Further, Hebrews 11:37-40 reveals even more of the hardships the saints of old endured. We and our sons may need to endure them as well.

> They were stoned, they were sawn in two, were tempted, were slain with the sword. They wandered about in sheepskins and goatskins, being destitute, afflicted, tormented of whom the world was not worthy. They wandered in deserts and

mountains, in dens and caves of the earth. And all these, having obtained a good testimony through faith, did not receive the promise, God having provided something better for us, that they should not be made perfect apart from us.

We look, instead, for our heavenly home:

For we know that if our earthly house, this tent, is destroyed, we have a building from God, a house not made with hands, eternal in the heavens. For in this we groan, earnestly desiring to be clothed with our habitation which is from heaven, if indeed, having been clothed, we shall not be found naked. For we who are in this tent groan, being burdened, not because we want to be unclothed, but further clothed, that mortality may be swallowed up by life. Now He who has prepared us for this very thing is God, who also has given us the Spirit as a guarantee. So we are always confident, knowing that while we are at home in the body we are absent from the Lord. For we walk by faith, not by sight. (2 Corinthians 5:1-7)

"Son, This World is Not Your Home"

53

EVERY SON NEEDS TO HEAR
HIS FATHER SAY:
"Son, Pull Your Weight"

If the whole body were an eye, where would be the hearing? If the whole were hearing, where would be the smelling? But now God has set the members, each one of them, in the body just as He pleased.

- 1 Corinthians 12:17-18

CHAPTER 4
DIVISION OF LABOR

In order to have a productive work life, a boy must understand the doctrine of division of labor, for he must learn to play his God-ordained part.

Iwo Jima was a grand theatre where division of labor was put on display. For example, I was shocked when my father told me that he never fired a shot on the island of Iwo Jima. He said it was not his job, for he was on a completely different mission than the United States Marine Corps or the Navy or the Seabees. He was not supposed to kill Japanese defenders on Iwo Jima and was actually ordered to stay out of the way. He was ordered to fly airplanes with the goal to bring Japan to its knees through an air war. He had his focus, while other men had theirs. However, they were not disconnected from one another; their unique perspectives, their professional specialties for their collaborative counsel, were operating in a unified effort.

Every man had a job on Iwo Jima: the Navy brought the men and supplies to the beach and shuttled the wounded; the Marine Corps secured the island through hand-to-hand combat; the Seabees built the airfields, roads, and command posts; the Army Air Corps protected the island from aerial attack and launched fighter strikes to protect B-29s on their bombing raids of mainland Japan.

It was an epic team effort. All were needed. If one of the teams had been pulled out of the conflict, the whole operation would have fallen apart. Strength was distributed throughout the various roles and responsibilities. As each man performed his unique function, mutual support created a greater, unified strength.

This division of labor produced a devastating defeat of Japan. The invasion and control of Iwo Jima made it possible for the United States Army Air Force to destroy sixty-five major Japanese cities before dropping the atomic bombs which finally ended the war.

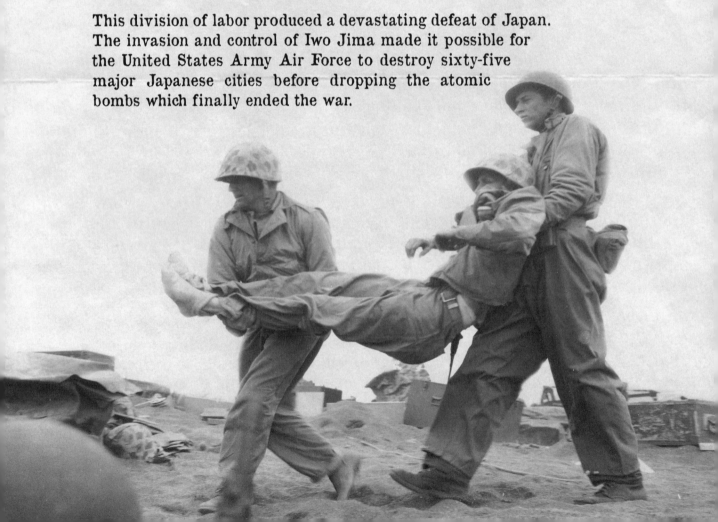

By the time we dropped the atomic bombs, the strength of the Japanese empire was deflated and the "Rising Sun" was setting fast. Our bombing raids had plunged Japan hopelessly into the most extreme conditions imaginable. We leveled her cities, ruined her factories, destroyed her transportation systems, and eliminated her air force and navy. By the summer of 1945, there was no competition in the air or on the sea from Japanese forces while the Grim Reapers of hunger and privation dogged every Japanese citizen.

IT TAKES COORDINATION TO DO GREAT THINGS.

The powerful results of this division of labor exemplify the power of men working together. It takes men in coordination to accomplish great things. There must be authority and submission as well as division of labor and flexibility.

This principle is true for the most important areas of life—church, home, and government. In the church there are different gifts among the members ("hands and feet") and different offices like elders and deacons, each with its own responsibilities and duties. Scripture requires that men and women fill different roles in the church (1 Corinthians 12:4-11, Titus 1-2). In the home, a godly division of labor is necessary for the building of a home life that is pleasing to God and a blessing to the community. There are different roles and responsibilities given to husband and wife that, when they are working together in concert, produce a beautiful home life (Ephesians 5:22-33). Civil government also plays its unique role in punishing evildoers (Romans 13:4).

All of these arenas require a division of labor that fits in the framework of the wisdom of God and they are all defined and regulated in Scripture so that we don't have to make up life as we go. There is a divine pattern.

WISE MEN UNDERSTAND THEY CANNOT DO IT ALL — THEY NEED OTHER MEN.

The most effective men are not wise in their own eyes so they seek the counsels of the wisest. In addition, no man has all the skills necessary to make his way through life, so it is important that he be humble enough to be able to identify superior skill in the lives of other men and work with them in unity, each one serving the others for the glory of God.

A wise, coordinated division of labor is unstoppable, and our labors are more effective when we work together. Solomon put it this way:

> For by wise counsel you will wage your own war, and in a multitude of counselors there is safety (Proverbs 24:6).

The apostle Paul communicated this anti-individualistic idea to the members of the church in Corinth. He wanted them to understand the church is like a body with many members, each performing different, and important, functions.

> For in fact the body is not one member but many. If the foot should say, "Because I am not a hand, I am not of the body," is it therefore not of the body? And if the ear should say, "Because I am not an eye, I am not of the body," is it therefore not of the body? If the whole body were an eye, where would be the hearing? If the whole were hearing, where would be the smelling? But now God has set the members, each one of them, in the body just as He pleased. And if they were all one member, where

would the body be? But now indeed there are many members, yet one body. And the eye cannot say to the hand, "I have no need of you"; nor again the head to the feet, "I have no need of you." No, much rather, those members of the body which seem to be weaker are necessary. And those members of the body which we think to be less honorable, on these we bestow greater honor; and our unpresentable parts have greater modesty, but our presentable parts have no need. But God composed the body, having given greater honor to that part which lacks it, that there should be no schism in the body, but that the members should have the same care for one another. And if one member suffers, all the members suffer with it; or if one member is honored, all the members rejoice with it (I Corinthians 12:14-26).

Moses learned this lesson battling against the Amalekites. Aaron and Hur came to his aid and their assistance caused the Israelites to be victorious in battle. If Moses' arms were not held up by his brothers, it would have meant disaster. I am sure his understanding of his dependence on his brothers was increased that day.

But Moses' hands became heavy; so they took a stone and put it under him, and he sat on it. And Aaron and Hur supported his hands, one on one side, and the other on the other side; and his hands were steady until the going down of the sun. (Exodus 17:12)

In this scene we notice the appreciation that Moses, Aaron and Hur had for one another as they helped each another accomplish the work of God. This clear picture stands in contrast to envy and grasping and dissatisfaction.

A Father Must

1. BEWARE OF ENVY.

It is easy to diminish your contribution in your own mind because of envy or dissatisfaction—or fear that the other guy will get all the glory.

There are some dramatic examples in Scripture of people who despised the role of others and suffered greatly for it. Miriam refused to accept the division of labor that God established for the wilderness wanderings, and God punished her with leprosy. Korah also rejected God's division of labor and it caused him and many others to be swallowed up in the earth under the wrath of God. Numbers 16:30 tells us the root cause of Korah's rebellion,

> But if the Lord creates a new thing, and the earth opens its mouth and swallows them up with all that belongs to them, and they go down alive into the pit, then you will understand that these men have rejected the Lord.

It was not Moses he was rejecting; it was the Lord and the division of labor He established. Miriam and Korah desired something different from what the Lord provided and it caused them to rise up against Moses, the one whom God had chosen.

2. TRAIN A HAPPY AND HARMONIOUS WORKER.

Unhappiness with our station often makes us unable to work in harmony with the others with whom God has put us. The apostle Paul himself "learned in whatever state I am, to be content" (Philippians 4:11). Contentment with what God has provided helps harmony flourish. It is good medicine and it makes work seem easier and go more quickly.

3. HELP HIS SON REJOICE IN DIFFERENCES.

God has ordained that we are not all the same nor do we play identical roles in life. The multiplicity of giftedness that God spreads out is wondrous and the best thing to do is to simply marvel and rejoice and refrain from getting bitter. Many workers spend valuable years pining away because God has not given them certain gifts, but God is sovereign in the particular gifts he gave us. Wise men rejoice in the differences and will not envy men who are equipped to do a different job.

4. EXPLAIN THAT PERSONAL OBEDIENCE IS OFTEN REQUIRED FOR THE GOOD ACCOMPLISHMENT OF THE WHOLE.

As previously discussed, the transformation of Mt. Suribachi was not only a direct result of courageous, visionary leadership, it was also the result of the personal obedience of soldiers faithfully carrying out their orders, often against their personal inclinations.

5. DEMONSTRATE THE IMPORTANCE OF GATHERING A WIDE BASE OF COUNSEL.

Solomon communicated the importance of this in this way, "Plans are established by counsel; by wise counsel wage war" (Proverbs 20:18).

Godly counsel is the key. "My people ask counsel from their wooden idols, and their staff informs them. For the spirit of harlotry has caused them to stray, and they have played the harlot against their God" (Hosea 4:12).

6. COACH HIS SON TO PLAY HIS PART WITH ALL HIS MIGHT AND TRUST GOD WITH THE RESULTS.

In God's economy each one has a particular function to perform, but if anyone in the chain is weak or irresponsible the whole will be affected. This is why boys need to learn to exert themselves with all their hearts. Carry your weight with joy in your heart, work in harmony, do not despise the labors of others and know that God will see to it that you do not live in vain.

Helping a boy to pull his own weight happens when we help him to understand the principles of how to work with other people, the importance of acknowledging and appreciating the contributions of others, how to play his part, and that his labors can be multiplied if he is able to work harmoniously with others.

"Son, Pull Your Weight"

EVERY SON NEEDS TO HEAR
HIS FATHER SAY:

"Son, Repent and Believe in the Gospel"

Therefore, since we are receiving a kingdom which cannot be shaken, let us have grace, by which we may serve God acceptably with reverence and godly fear. For our God is a consuming fire.

- Hebrews 12:28-29

CHAPTER 5
THE TERRORS OF FLAMETHROWERS

A son can receive and follow all kinds of moral lessons of manhood from his father, but if he does not embrace the gospel, his "character" will do him no eternal good. It may make him a nicer and more successful guy here on earth, but it won't help him deal with his greatest problem—his lostness before a holy God and the threat of eternal fire. After all, many nice boys are sent to hell because they did not escape the wrath to come. Fire is one of the prominent images the Bible uses to communicate how radically vital this is. The use of flamethrowers on Iwo Jima during the battle gives us an illustration of the nature of fire, and the importance of escaping it.

You cannot understand the battle for Iwo Jima without understanding flamethrowers. This is because we had an enemy largely unaffected by bombs and bullets, but they could be destroyed with fire hurtling through the air licking up everything in its path.

The flamethrower is helpful in illustrating the horrors of eternal fire. This is one of the motivations God gives us to help us understand that we ought to turn to Him.

On Iwo, Jima, we learned that most of our bombing efforts were in vain. The Japanese were dug in so deep, they escaped death even though they were pounded by the heaviest pre-invasion bombing in the history of the Pacific war.

Not only was bombing ineffective, but bullets had their limitations as well. Bullets were ineffective because the enemy was hidden in caves and concealed bunkers. They would pop up and then disappear, running underground to another cave opening, repeating this over and over.

The United States Marines on Iwo Jima were constantly facing off with impregnable concrete bunkers full of gunners who were able to retreat to the safety of tunnels behind them. The flamethrower was the perfect weapon to neutralize these positions. It is hard to conceive of a more frightening weapon of war and the psychological effects were powerful.

Imagine yourself as a Japanese soldier holed up in a cave, and a roaring sound thunders toward you. You have been playing sniper in your protected bunker. You have retreated to the safety of the cave. Suddenly, you feel the heat on your face, and then you cannot breathe because the flames have consumed the oxygen, and then you pass out. You never saw your enemy, but you were forced to understand some measure of "consuming fire."

The flamethrower was the modern, twentieth century equivalent of dropping boiling oil on the enemy.

If you are looking for a "humane" weapon, this is not one of them. It was chemical warfare pure and simple; a most terrorizing weapon of war.

The portable backpack flamethrower consisted of two tanks that fed into one nozzle. In one tank there was a mix of two-thirds diesel fuel, one-third one hundred octane gasoline, and napalm jelly. The other tank was filled with compressed gas. When the valves merging the fuel and gas opened up, liquid flame blasted through the nozzle, burning anything within 100 feet. The Marines used the third revision of the flamethrower, the eighty pound M2-2. It was the most effective weapon on Iwo Jima.

My friend and Marine on Iwo, Bill Henderson told me, "We could not have taken the island without the flamethrower." My dad said that "the flame-thrower saved lives because the weapon did not require solders to go inside the cave to get the enemy. The caves were booby-trapped and promised certain death for all who entered."

The flamethrower was an effective weapon, but the job was no picnic. Here are a few reasons it was a difficult weapon to use:

Its bulky, heavy package made it hard to run with on rough terrain;

If the wind changed and blew the flames back on you—you were toast;

It was slow and hard getting up from lying on the ground wearing the backpack.

Apart from these physical difficulties, there was one major downside: anyone carrying one had a short lifespan. One flamethrower unit on Iwo had a 92% casualty rate. A Marine who trained flamethrower operators there told me he thought that the average lifespan of the flamethrower operator was around four minutes.

The short life expectancy was due to two facts. First, flamethrowers were so successfully used in destroying bunker positions that the Japanese feared and hated them above any other weapon. Second, flamethrower operators were carrying bulky, heavy tanks of explosive fuel on their backs, making them marked men—easy to see and easy to hit and easy to blow up. Carrying a flamethrower was like putting a giant bull's eye on your back that said, "Hit me here." The danger to the operator was huge. This is why many of the flamethrower pictures from Iwo Jima also show other soldiers covering the flamethrower operator. These men were strapping on a backpack of explosives and putting themselves in front of a hail of gunfire. I think they call this courage.

Only a few flamethrower operators lived to tell their stories. Imagine the difficulty of trying to get testimonies from men who actually handled flame-throwers. Problem: They are all dead. Well, almost all. One who survived was Corporal Hershel "Woody" Williams of Quiet Dell, West Virginia. Williams' heroics as a flamethrower operator in the battle for Iwo Jima would earn him the Medal of Honor, one of twenty-seven awarded to United States Marines who fought on Iwo. Today, the retired buck sergeant is one of only three living Medal of Honor recipients from Iwo Jima. "It was like fighting ghosts," he says. "One minute the enemy was attacking and being killed, then they would disappear, including their dead. They were going underground into 16 miles of tunnels we didn't know existed."[1]

Because flamethrowers were so dangerous to soldiers who carried them, we began mounting them on tanks, thus reducing the casualty rates. The tank units used the same basic technology, except their range was longer—150 feet—and flame duration was longer.

In the words of Captain Frank C. Caldwell, a company commander in the 26th Marines: "In my view it was the flame tank more than any other supporting arm that won this battle." Tactical demands for the flame tanks never diminished. Late in the battle, as the 5th Marine Division cornered the last Japanese defenders in "The Gorge," the 5th Tank Battalion expended napalm-thickened fuel at the rate of 10,000 gallons per day. The division's final action report stated that the flame tank was "the one weapon that caused the Japs to leave their caves and rock crevices and run."[2]

The flamethrower calls up dreaded images of burning to death in a fiery furnace of thousands of degrees of life-consuming heat.

These images remind us of the way fire is used in the Bible to explain the nature of the judgment of God against sin. They help us to see how irrational it is to reject God in the face of the unavoidable consequences. God is a consuming fire who judges sinners with righteous judgment and punishes them with fire.

His Word is like a fire; His judgment is with fire; He is a consuming fire.

Because there is no place to hide, the wise would run to Him for mercy.

> The Lord reigns, let the earth rejoice...A fire goes before Him, and burns up His enemies round about. (Psalm 97:1)

> "Therefore I have poured out My indignation on them; I have consumed them with the fire of My wrath; and I have recompensed their deeds on their own heads," says the Lord God. (Ezekiel 22:31)

> So it will be at the end of the age. The angels will come forth, separate the wicked from among the just, and cast them into the furnace of fire. There will be wailing and gnashing of teeth. (Matthew 13:49-50)

Escaping the wrath to come involves embracing the gospel by coming before a Holy God, and repenting of sin and following Christ.

A Father Must

1. PREACH THE GOSPEL TO HIS SON.

This is the most important thing a father will ever do. It is a father's responsibility to preach the whole counsel of God to his son so that he knows who he is, who God is, and what God requires of His creatures. Every Boy needs instruction concerning God, sin, the law, hell and judgment, the new birth, grace, repentance, faith, and salvation through Christ alone. I would encourage fathers to help their children understand these categories as they are listed below with Scripture references.

GOD

1. 1 John 4:8,16. God is Love.

2. Exodus. 34:6-7. God is Merciful.

3. Revelation 29:11-15. God is a Judge.

SIN

1. Genesis 2:15-17. Adam and Eve's disobedience resulted in death.

2. Romans 6:23. The wages of sin is death.

3. Romans 3:23. Everyone is a sinner.

THE LAW

1. Exodus 20:1-20. The Ten Commandments must be obeyed perfectly.

2. Matthew 22:34-40. If we disobey the first and second greatest commandments, we have broken all of the Bible's laws.

3. James 2:10-11. If we break one commandment we've broken them all.

HELL AND JUDGMENT

1. Revelation 20:11-15. The Great White Throne Judgment.

2. Matthew 25:41-46. Everlasting fire and punishment for the unsaved.

3. Hebrews 9:27. After this life comes judgment.

THE NEW BIRTH

1. John 3:1-7. Jesus teaches that the "new birth" is necessary for salvation.

2. John 1:13. Salvation is not inherited from our parents or secured by our effort.

3. 2 Corinthians 5:17. To be born again means that our old life is replaced by a new one.

GRACE

1. Ephesians 2:8,9. Grace is unmerited favor.

2. Acts 15:11. We are saved by the grace of Christ.

3. Romans 4:3-5. Salvation is by grace through faith and not by the deeds of the law.

REPENTANCE

I. Luke 13:3. Unless we repent, we will all perish.

2. Acts 3:19. We must repent and be converted.

3. Matthew 4:17. Jesus said, "Repent, for the kingdom of heaven is at hand."

FAITH

1. Hebrews 11:6. Without faith it is impossible to please God.

2. John 20:24-29. Blessed are they who do not see, yet believe.

3. John 3:16-19. Whoever believes in Him will not perish but have eternal life.

SALVATION THROUGH CHRIST ALONE

1. John 14:6. Jesus is the way, the truth, and the life.

2. 1 John 5:11-13. He that has the Son has life.

3. John 3:36. He who does not believe on the Son of God has the wrath of God on him.[3]

"Son, Repent and Believe in the Gospel"

EVERY SON NEEDS TO HEAR

HIS FATHER SAY:

"Son, Arm Yourself with the Right Weapons"

Put on the whole armor of God, that you may be able to stand against the wiles of the devil. For we do not wrestle against flesh and blood, but against principalities, against powers, against the rulers of the darkness of this age, against spiritual hosts of wickedness in the heavenly places. Therefore take up the whole armor of God, that you may be able to withstand in the evil day, and having done all, to stand.

- Ephesians 6:11-13

Chapter 6
THE P-51D MUSTANG

The P-51 Mustang was my father's weapon of war on Iwo Jima. Helping sons choose the best weapons for the battles they will face is one of the most important things a father will ever do.

My appreciation for this plane is why I have a large, imposing picture of one in my office. When people see it, the most common comment they make is, "That is a beautiful plane." One of my friends calls this airplane "Industrial Art."

The P-51 is one of the most collectible airplanes in the history of aviation; collectors are willing to part with big dollars to find and restore them.

The Mustang was one of the most important planes in World War II. The Senate War Investigating Committee in 1944 said that the Mustang was "The most aerodynamically perfect pursuit plane in existence."[1]

General H.H. "Hap" Arnold said, "One of the great miracles of the war was the fact that the long range (Mustang) fighter escort did appear over Germany at just the saving moment."[2]

Major General Orvil Anderson, Deputy Commanding Officer of the Eighth Air Force, said, "It is my considered opinion that the P51 played a decisive role in the air war over Western Europe."[3]

"That's the plane I want!" said General Carl Spaatz, Commanding Officer of the Eighth Air Force, seeing the Mustang production line.[4]

Perhaps the most telling statement of all is this one by Hermann Goering on March 4, 1944: "When I saw (Mustang) fighters escorting the bombers over Berlin, I knew the jig was up."[5]

Of the various iterations of the P51 Mustang, the P51D "is generally accepted as the definitive Mustang."[6]

That was the plane my dad flew. 9,603 of them rolled off the assembly line and they were without question the finest fighter planes in World War II. In 1945, nearly the entire USAAF stable of fighter pilots flew P51 Ds. They were used in the Korean War, and the Israelis used them in 1956 to protect themselves during the Suez Crisis. They considered the P51 the most superior plane of their conflict.

It was a high-performance aircraft in a class of its own. It could climb fast and it gave the pilot superior acceleration during dogfights. A gun camera operated when the guns discharged.

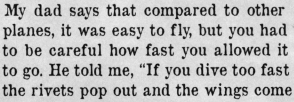

I've always been captivated by the Mustang. Its monster horsepower made it one of the fastest fighter planes in the air and it was high on maneuverability and performance. Its beautiful form is unmatched.

My dad says that compared to other planes, it was easy to fly, but you had to be careful how fast you allowed it to go. He told me, "If you dive too fast the rivets pop out and the wings come off. When diving you have to pull out gradually. In the P47 you can dive it steep, but not in a P-51, as the plane will dismember in the air."

The first time my father flew P51s was at Bellows Field in Hawaii. He tells me that on Bellows Field there was a guy in training who flew the plane too fast and made too violent a maneuver, causing the plane to fly apart—an important lesson for young bucks ready to take on the world.

He tells about how it also happened to another flyer in his squadron:

One of the better pilots in the 15th Fighter Group was on a mission east of Tokyo. He spotted a fake fighter on the ground, and dove in. His wing man dove with him, and he saw the flight leader's plane coming apart. The wing man eased off, but when he landed back on Iwo he found that most of his rivets had popped out. He was dangerously close to flying apart as well.

My dad really liked flying the P51. He said that a flight in the P47 was like trying to fly a wrench, while the P51 was like an arrow. He called the P47 a "bucket of bolts."

"MY PLANE WAS BETTER THAN YOUR PLANE"

When we visited Iwo Jima, we were sitting in a troop truck with some other men when I heard a startling comment pass the lips of my father. He was sitting next to another flyboy who had flown P47 Thunderbolts on Iwo Jima. My dad turned to him and said, "My plane was better than your plane." We all cracked up with laughter.

WHY DO BOYS LOVE SWORDS AND GUNS AND FIRES?

The good news is that most fathers get a jump-start on communicating this because, for some strange reason, most boys love weapons. Hand a five-year-old a banana and it becomes a revolver. A peanut butter and jelly sandwich is intuitively chewed into the shape of a pistol. Any stick becomes a knife or a sword. Perhaps the fact that weapons matter even to little boys comes from an innate understanding that having the right weapon for the right moment is critical for success in life.

The kind of weapon you have matters. For example, it would be silly to engage in aerial dogfights using swords and it would be equally silly to do hand-to-hand combat with squirt guns. These are overblown analogies, but they do help us think about using the right weapon for the right kind of battle. The right weapons are critical for the success of any battle. For example, the P51 Mustang was exactly what the war effort needed. Wars are won or lost on the choices that follow the command, "Gentlemen, choose your weapons." In WWII, my father's weapon was a P51 Mustang. What is your's? What will be your son's?

A Father Must

1. SHOW THAT THE BEST WEAPONS ARE NOT MADE OF STEEL.

It is not physical weapons that boys need the most, for God has promised that He is the defining factor in warfare: "I will not save them by bow nor by sword or battle, by horses or horsemen" (Hosea 1:7). 2 Samuel 1:27 records an incident where there was a failure of physical weapons, "How the mighty have fallen and the weapons of war perished." Scripture emphasizes dependence upon God rather than our own strength:

> No king is saved by the multitude of an army; a mighty man is not delivered by great strength. (Psalm 33:16)

> For the weapons of our warfare are not carnal but mighty in God for pulling down strongholds. (2 Corinthians 10:4)

> The Lord has opened His armory, and has brought out the weapons of his indignation; for this is the work of the Lord God of hosts in the land of the Chaldeans. (Jeremiah 50:25)

> Then David said to the Philistine, "You come to me with a sword, with a spear, and with a javelin. But I come to you in the name of the Lord of hosts, the god of the armies of Israel whom you have defied...then all this assembly shall know that the Lord does not save with sword or spear; for the battle is the Lord's and He will give you into our hands." (1 Samuel 17:45, 47)

Take your son to the Word of God.

THE BEST WEAPON OF ALL

In John Bunyan's Pilgrim's Progress, Valiant for Truth headed for the Celestial City and was attacked by three men, Wild Head, Inconsiderate, and Pragmatic. After hearing Valiant for Truth's story, Great Heart (Pilgrim's guide), asks about the weapon he used to withstand his enemies. Every boy needs to know what kind of weapon to use when "Wild Head" shows up, when "Inconsiderate" appears, and when "Pragmatic" speaks to him. What will a boy do when these personalities rise up? In the story, Valiant used the Word of God—that "Right Jerusalem Blade"[7]—that gets sharper and sharper with use. Here Bunyan helps us to understand how important it is to choose holy weapons. Boys will be attacked by various kinds of personalities all their lives long, just like Pilgrim. His best weapon, his ost trusted weapon, is the Word of God.

> For the Word of God is quick and powerful and sharper than any two edged sword, piercing even to the dividing asunder of soul and spirit, and of the joints and marrow, and is a discerner of the thoughts and intents of the heart." (Hebrews 4:12)

2. TEACH THEIR SONS HOW TO SELECT THE RIGHT WEAPONS FOR THE BATTLE.

A wise and godly man does not grab any old weapon at hand. He does not find his weapon in his own heart or out of his own words or out of his own established family culture. There is a right way and wrong way to respond. Some weapons are demonic and others are divine. The temptation with which we are always faced is the inclination to come up with our own weapons. When you are faced with a "hothead" or a "wild head," the temptation is to use a wild, hot headed weapon. When we are faced by inconsiderate people, we are tempted to use a weapon in kind. But, no matter how creative we might become in conceiving how we might fight our battles, we must always return to the principle that guidance by the Word of God is the only way for victory. Fathers need to help their sons have faith in the weapons God gives—not fleshly weapons against the hotheads or the unwise of the day, but heavenly weapons. They are the weapons of God's selection.

Boys need to know their weapons, sharpen the right ones and trust that God has given us all we need to wage the great wars of our time.

3. PRIORITIZE THE WEAPONS THAT ARE AVAILABLE.

When Solomon was a boy, God gave him the opportunity of a lifetime—to get whatever he asked of the Lord. He did not ask for earthly riches or worldly weapons of war or armies. He did not desire steel. He asked for wisdom, and that choice made all the difference. The years passed, and after a long life the queen of Sheba came to see the riches of Solomon. She left saying, "They did not tell me the half of his riches." After living a long life of unparalleled abundance, Solomon wrote, "Wisdom is better than weapons of war" (Ecclesiastes 9:18).

Even as a boy, Solomon understood how choosing the right weapon makes all the difference in the world (2 Chronicles 1:7).

Every boy understands how important weapons are. Perhaps that is why they love to carry them wherever they go. The most effective way a father can give his son the best weapons is to carry them himself, display them and use them in daily life. Deuteronomy 6:7 says that a father must "talk of them when he sits in his house, when he walks by the way, when he lies down and when he rises up." In doing so, a father fortifies the soul of his son with armaments that he will take with him wherever he may go.

```
        "Son, Arm Yourself with
            the Right Weapons"
```

EVERY SON NEEDS TO HEAR
HIS FATHER SAY:

"Son, Take on Mighty Challenges"

Who through faith subdued kingdoms, wrought righteousness, obtained promises, stopped the mouths of lions, quenched the violence of fire, escaped the edge of the sword, out of weakness were made strong, waxed valiant in fight, turned to flight the armies of the aliens.

- Hebrews 11:33-34

CHAPTER 7
MASSIVE DEPLOYMENT

The coordinated work effort for the massive deployment demonstrated during the battle for Iwo Jima teaches lessons that are reflective of the teaching of Scripture regarding a boy's work life, which forms the habits of the man he is becoming. A father must communicate these lessons to his son if he is going to be involved in meaningful labor for the glory of God.

Those who were involved in the battle for Iwo Jima engaged in a Herculean effort that was the epitome of stress, fatigue, and gigantic labor. The battle for Iwo Jima was a logistical effort executed four thousand miles away from its planners. These planners sent 80,000 troops across the ocean to a small, two-mile-wide by five-mile-long island, six hundred miles from the nearest mainland. It required over eight hundred ships to make it happen.

This was without question one of the most difficult and complex deployments in the history of warfare. And, this is the kind of immense conflict for which we ought to prepare our sons.

The preparations took on almost mythological proportions; the Marine Fifth Division alone had enough food to feed the population of Atlanta, Georgia for a month. There were 1,322 pounds of supplies and equipment for each of the 70,000 assault troops. And get this, the Marines alone brought "100,000,000 cigarettes." Yes, that's one hundred million.[1]

They brought water, morphine, fuel, grease, spare parts, carburetor rebuild kits, blood plasma, paper and pencils, portable airstrips and Marsden Plates (roads), bandages, rope, maps, tires, bullets, batteries, Bibles, cooking supplies, K-rations, C-rations, dog food, garbage cans, welding rods, asphalt, flashlights, flares, blankets, toilet paper, socks, underwear, and my father's personal favorite—Hershey chocolate bars by the hundreds of thousands.

Colonel Joseph Alexander described the challenges this way, "Iwo Jima represented at once the supreme test and the pinnacle of American am-

phibious capabilities in the Pacific War."[2] It was a build-up that even Hollywood could never reproduce.

On February 19, at 9:00 a.m., Admiral Turner ordered, "LAND THE LANDING FORCE!"

And, what a force it was!

The landing force was a tightening noose of ships that went seven miles out from the island as three Marine divisions were landing. Even though the wind whipped up and made for some dangerous landing conditions, they kept on coming.

There were fleets of tank landing ships (LSTs) filled with amphibious tanks and "alligators," there were medium landing ships (LSMs), there were smaller landing craft tanks (LCTs) and packs of infantry landing craft (LCIs) gathering about the island.

The ring of ships was drawing tighter. Small boats were moving out

bearing flags to mark the rallying points from which the landing waves would deploy.

The logistical problems were so great that the Japanese wagered we wouldn't try an invasion because of the difficulty. They were dead wrong.

They underestimated both our resolve and the largeness of the scale with which we were prepared to operate. What they discovered was a massive deployment beyond their expectations.

God forbid that we would allow our boys to be lazy pleasure-seekers who only love to hang out, play games, and produce nothing. We live in a day and age where people are looking for a stress-free life of leisure. The modern heart wants to escape pain and fatigue at all costs and so we say "amen" to the message, "You deserve a break today." This message does not serve us well, and it must be remembered that there is another way to live—the biblical way. Boys need to be prepared from their youth to be ready to expend great efforts for their families, churches, and nations.

A Father Must

1. EXTOL THE THE ENERGY REQUIRED FOR GREAT ACCOMPLISHMENTS.

First, let's communicate to our sons that great energy is usually required for great deeds. In all warfare and in all of life it is necessary to make great preparations, work with all our hearts, and remember that "He who has a slack hand becomes poor, But the hand of the diligent makes rich" (Proverbs 10:4). Lest we keep thinking only on an earthly plane, we ought to remind ourselves that the most glorious accomplishment in all of history was accomplished through endurance:

> Let us run with endurance the race that is set before us, looking unto Jesus the author and finisher of our faith; who for the joy that was set before Him endured the cross, despising the shame, and is sat down at the right hand of the throne of

God. For consider Him that endured such contradiction of sinners against himself, lest ye be wearied and faint in your minds. Ye have not yet resisted unto blood, striving against sin. (Hebrews 12:1-4)

2. EXORCISE THEIR FEAR OF GREAT EFFORT.

This second lesson exposes the most common barrier that people face in doing anything of importance—the fear of great effort. So many important projects are never started because people are afraid of hardship and persevering labors. They get a great idea and then shirk back because it looks too big and will require too much of them. There is an undercurrent running in the souls of most of us that goes like this: "If it is easy, it must be right; if it is hard, it must be wrong." A Christian might put it this way, "If it is effortless, it must be of the Lord." I have known a number of people who have recoiled from starting companies and churches and many other pursuits because they were afraid of what it would cost them in time, effort and difficulty.

Boys should be filled up with the knowledge that God is Almighty and that they have no reason to fear failure. The greatest deeds are accomplished only when fear is banished by faith. The Lord desired to banish this same kind of fear in the spirit of Jeremiah for He said, "Behold, I am the Lord, the God of all flesh. Is there anything too hard for Me?" (Jeremiah 32:26-28).

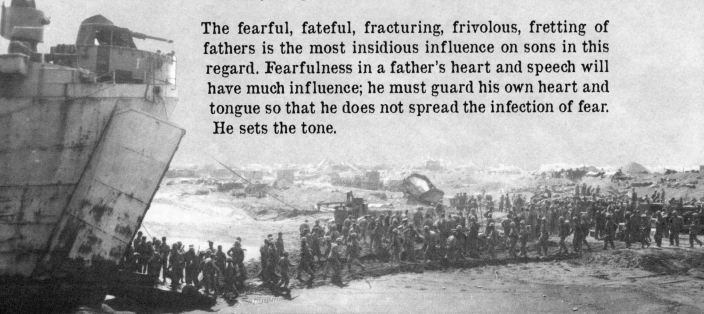

The fearful, fateful, fracturing, frivolous, fretting of fathers is the most insidious influence on sons in this regard. Fearfulness in a father's heart and speech will have much influence; he must guard his own heart and tongue so that he does not spread the infection of fear. He sets the tone.

3. EXHORT SONS TO EMBRACE SUFFERING AS NECESSARY FOR A GREATER GOOD.

James explains, "My brethren, take the prophets, who spoke in the name of the Lord, as an example of suffering and patience" (James 5:10).

Paul, who understood fatigue and hardship and poured out his life as a drink offering, said, "For I consider that the sufferings of this present time are not worthy to be compared with the glory which shall be revealed in us" (Romans 8:18).

When a father comes through the door after a hard day at work, his countenance tells all. Is he rejoicing in his sufferings as a necessary good, or does he come in dragging and complaining and obsessing about his need for relaxation?

4. EXPLAIN THE STORIES OF THE GREAT EFFORTS GIVEN IN SCRIPTURE.

This is how our great heroes of the faith functioned: Noah built an ark, Moses took millions of people through forty years in the desert, and Joseph labored for fourteen years providing for the starving people of Egypt and the surrounding countries.

We don't want boys to grow up like Peter Pan, but like Paul who was so engaged in his work in the gospel that he would glory in his sufferings to the point of saying, "I had no rest in my spirit" (2 Corinthians 2:13).

Fathers must read their sons the stories in Scripture that catalog the great efforts displayed there.

5. EXPOSE SONS TO THE TRUTH THAT THE BATTLE BELONGS TO THE LORD WHILE THE AVAILABILITY AND EFFORT BELONG TO US.

> The preparations of the heart belong to man, but the answer of the tongue is from the Lord. (Proverbs 16:1)

> Faith without works is dead (James 2:17).

Let's be men like this, engaging in great deeds that involve great effort. Let's not be the kind of men who settle for small projects that require little effort and make little difference. We shouldn't allow our children to waste their lives hanging out, playing games, and being entertained. Let's take them with us into the great projects God has given us. Let's get them early into high-stakes accomplishments. Let's do something that matters, even if it might be HARD!

"Son, Take on Mighty Challenges"

EVERY SON NEEDS TO HEAR
HIS FATHER SAY:

"Son, Trust in the Sovereign Hand of God"

I know that You can do all things, and that no purpose of
Yours can be thwarted.

- Job 42:2

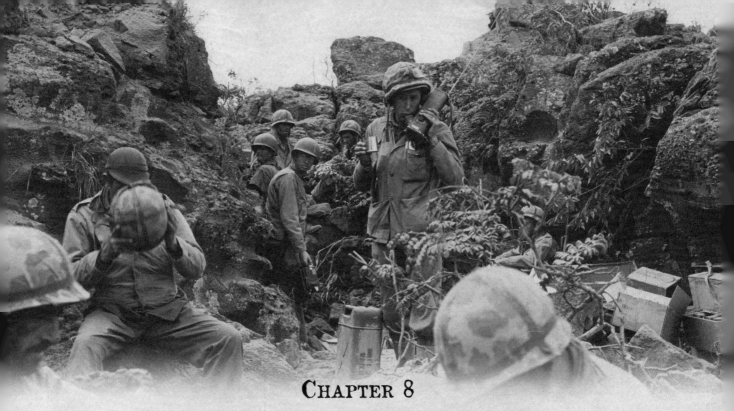

CHAPTER 8
HANDLING DIRE STRAITS

How will you help your boy look back on the trials and the sometimes monstrous situations he will experience? If he is going to succeed, a father must help his son get his doctrine in order. A boy must know the God of the Bible—the true God who knows the number of the hairs on his head, his thoughts before he thinks them, and his steps before he takes them. He must know the God who is sovereign over all of His creation.

When difficulties arise, the normal human reaction is to cultivate blame, bitterness, and regret and to see oneself as a victim. This happens because of the common temptations to sin which accompany trials. It is here, in our weakness, where the Devil may be able to storm the doors of our hearts, for the history of our lives is often littered with incomprehensible situations that sometimes include the evil actions of other people.

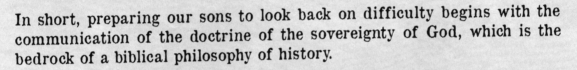

How do you prepare sons
for a life where looming
threats so large and evil
are clearly at work? How
do we respond to this world
in which we are strangers in a
strange land, in which lies in the
power of the evil one (1 John 5:19),
this world where "that serpent of old,
called the Devil and Satan, deceives
the whole world" (Revelation 12:9).

In short, preparing our sons to look back on difficulty begins with the communication of the doctrine of the sovereignty of God, which is the bedrock of a biblical philosophy of history.

A person's philosophy of history is of enormous significance. Whether one views history like a Marxist, or a Hindu, or a Christian, creates tremendous differences.

In the same way, a soldier's view of history will have a dramatic influence on how he understands the battle for Iwo Jima and all that took place there. If he looks back at that battle as a collection of chance events dictated by the whims, passions, and the powers of men, he will think about it in a fatalistic way. But if he looks at it with an awareness of the orchestrating sovereign hand of God, he will come away with different interpretations and convictions about God's purposes in that important event.

When our boys went ashore on Iwo Jima they met a ferocious enemy. The protective fanaticism of the Japanese during World War II can be documented in a number of ways. To put this into perspective we need first to remember that no foreign army had set foot on Japanese soil for 5,000 years. When Commodore Perry sailed into Tokyo Bay in 1853, he was very seriously and carefully rebuffed. Second, the Bushido Code ("Way of the Warrior") demanded "no survivors." For this reason, while 12,864 bodies of dead Japanese soldiers were counted on Iwo, only eighty-one soldiers surrendered, and forty-five of those were Koreans—they fought to the death. Third, the purpose of the battle for Iwo Jima, from a Japanese perspective, was to scare America away from its march toward Japan. The Japanese knew that much more was at stake than this small island. General Kuribiyashi believed that if he could kill enough Americans, Washington would reconsider the invasion of the Japanese mainland.

The Japanese soldiers on Iwo Jima knew that they were under a death sentence. They were told that they would never leave the island alive and therefore, they must each kill ten Americans before they perished. The enemy was in a death grip and everyone knew it. General Kuribiyashi spent some of his time writing letters to his family instructing them in the way they should go since he knew he would never return home. He had carefully reconciled himself to his own death.

Our troops also knew the internal conflicts that went with such devastating circumstances. According to General Graves Erskine, "Victory was never in doubt. Its cost was. What was in doubt, in all our minds, was whether there would be any of us left to dedicate our cemetery at the end, or whether the last Marine would die knocking out the last Japanese gunner."[1]

How should the boys who stormed the beaches of Iwo Jima look back upon such a terrible situation? They had to look back terror and heart wrenching choices and compromises that were forced upon them. What would be their view of the fanaticism of the enemy that they encountered on Iwo? What kinds of conclusions should they draw from such a barbaric experience? Many men dealt with it by stopping up their experiences inside themselves up for fifty years and never speaking about it. Others grew bitter against

the Japanese. Some were never able to shake it. Stories of this are myriad and common.

One thing is certain: If you maintain a truly biblical understanding of history, the difficult stories transform from dead-end tragedies. They are transformed by a sovereign God who oversees all and controls even the weather. Not only will they give you insight into the past but steadiness for today and hope for tomorrow.

Consider the amazing providences of God in the midst of the B-29 bombing raids:

My friend Buck Bunn recalls the amazing phenomenon that he was able to observe in these bombing raids. Those familiar with the history of warfare know that there are countless stories showing that small changes in the weather can make the difference between winning and losing. This was par-

ticularly true in the final year of WWII as strange wind patterns improved the effects of our bombing efforts.

The B-29 bombing raids against Japan were often exponentially effective because they were fueled by winds that whipped up just at the right time. Those winds caused massive firestorms that swept through the cities, destroying the infrastructure of the country, finally breaking Japan.

Just to give a statistical picture, consider the following facts.

Before the Enola Gay dropped the ultimate weapon of the war—the atomic bomb—we had already destroyed sixty-five of Japan's principal cities. Here is how the USAF describes the damage: "602 major war factories destroyed... 1,250,000 tons of shipping sunk by aerial mines...83% oil refinery production destroyed and 75% aircraft engine production destroyed...2,300,000 homes destroyed...330,000 killed...476,000 wounded." B-29 attacks resulted in more civilian casualties than the Japanese armed forces suffered in three-and-a-half years of war with the U.S. 8,500,000 people were rendered homeless and 21,000,000 were displaced.

Japan's largest cities were already in ruins when we dropped the bomb. It is startling to understand that 39% of Tokyo (the size of New York City) was completely destroyed, as well as 57% of Yokohama (the size of Cleveland); 55.7% of Kobe (the size of Baltimore); 44% of Nagoya (the size of Los Angeles); and 35% of Osaka (the size of Chicago).[2]

The B-29 was a fearsome weapon. An enemy who heard the roaring sounds of its engines overhead was stabbed in the heart with fear. And for good reason. They were big, they were loud, and they carried destruction in their wake.

And Buck was a B-29 bomber pilot.

Buck Bunn was just a boy when he became a B-29 pilot—seventeen years old. But it was Buck who led me to an amazing discovery about my father's

experience as a P51 Mustang pilot and taught me about the role of the B-29 in the Pacific War.

I met Buck as a result of a conversation I had with Bill Henderson; I met Bill Henderson because my friend Jim Dyer told me about him. It was a chain of events and relationships that only God could have linked together arranged. My meeting up with Buck happened as a result of a lunch I had with Bill one day. I asked if he knew any other men locally who had been on Iwo Jima. He said, "Buck Bunn was a B-29 pilot, and he lives right here in Raleigh."

So I called up Buck to see if he could get together with me. When my son and I met him for lunch I asked, "Buck, what were you doing on May 29, 1945?" I asked him because this was the day my dad was shot down while escorting B-29s on a bombing raid to Japan. He said, "I was on one of the biggest raids of the war over Yokohama."

I said "Really? My dad was flying a P51 Mustang on that raid, and he was shot down outside Tokyo Bay."

He replied, "No kidding! I saw a guy bail out of his P51 Mustang outside Tokyo Bay that day and have never forgotten it. I always wondered what happened to that guy. I thought that it may have been my gunner that shot him."

I thought, "Is it possible Buck Bunn saw my dad bail out of his plane on May 29?" And, what's more, "Could it have been Buck's gunner that shot my dad?"

I hurried home, got out my history books, and made some phone calls to see how many Mustangs went down on May 29, 1945. Here are my findings: this was the last long-range mission and the most tactically successful of that month. During a very heavy incendiary attack, two Mustangs were shot down. One was piloted by my father, who bailed out; the other guy's plane plummeted straight into the ocean and he was killed. That flyer was Rufus S. Moore.

One of the interesting puzzle pieces of my dad's story is that he was shot down by "friendly fire." The term describes an unintended attack from your own countrymen. In other words, my father was shot down by another American plane. Most likely, it was one of our own B-29s that shot my father down.

I was stunned at the thought that living right here in my hometown was the man who saw my father bail out of his P-51 Mustang. But it was even more amazing to think that Buck Bunn's gunner may have been the one who blew my father out of the sky: Buck's gunnery records show a kill on that day—friendly fire—on a P-51 Mustang.

Perhaps one of the truly interesting and humorous encounters I have ever seen took place on my farm, between Buck and my father. Fifty-nine years after the incident, the two men met for the first time and recalled the events of May 29, 1945. They laughed as the one pilot turned to the other with an apology—"Bill, I'm sorry if I shot you down," Bunn said.

"No problem," my dad replied. "Don't worry about it."

In the years since I met Buck, he has been a great source of information about the B-29, and he has even given a couple of lectures on the subject at our annual Memorial Day Picnic. He shared with us that Iwo Jima was a critical staging point for the final blows that brought the Japanese to surrender. The three airfields on the island of Iwo Jima were located in perfect position to make the final knock-out punch. None of our fighter planes was capable of the long trip from Saipan and Tinian to the Japanese mainland, but Iwo Jima's airfields brought them within range of protecting the long-range B-29s. The mission of the P-51 on these raids was to keep enemy fighter planes away from the B-29 bombers as they flew over their Japanese targets. This was a challenge since fanatical kamikaze pilots in Japanese Zeros would crash into the B-29s.

Since the B-29 bases were on Saipan and Tinian, the bombers would leave and head for Iwo Jima where the P-51 Mustangs would meet them in the air at ten thousand feet and escort them to Japanese targets.

Buck commented to me that it was remarkable to him that nearly every time they went on a mission to bomb Japanese cities, there would be a roaring wind that would arise unexpectedly to fan the flames the bombings generated, destroying much of the landscape. Sometimes the firestorms were so fierce that pilots reported that getting too close to the heat during a firestorm would make them lose control. Sometimes the rising hot air would turn the airplane upside down.

The equipment was available. The pilots were ready and able. The protective P-51 Mustangs were in position. But the final victory was from the Lord who took all of the resources under His command and controlled the weather, multiplying all the human effort beyond measure.

Scripture records instances where God controlled the winds. For example, in Egypt, He caused an east wind to arise and then he caused it to shift from the west,

> ... and the Lord brought an east wind on the land all that day and all that night. When it was morning, the east wind brought the locusts. And the locusts went up over all the land of Egypt and rested on all the territory of Egypt. They were very severe; previously there had been no such locusts as they, nor shall there be such after them. For they covered the face of the whole earth, so that the land was darkened; and they ate every herb of the land and all the fruit of the trees which the hail had left. So there remained nothing green on the trees or on the plants of the field throughout all the land of Egypt... And the Lord turned a very strong west wind, which took the locusts away and blew them into the Red Sea. There remained not one locust in all the territory of Egypt. But the Lord hardened Pharaoh's heart, and he did not let the children of Israel go. (Exodus 10:12-20)

We must realize, and we must help our sons realize, that the success of all our plans and stratagems are dependent upon the sovereignty of God. He controls the wind, the rain and the waves. He determines all outcomes, and we are but dust. The words of Proverbs 21:30-31 express this perfectly:

> There is no wisdom nor understanding nor counsel against the LORD. The horse is prepared against the day of battle: but safety is of the LORD.

There are hundreds of passages of Scripture defining the doctrine of the sovereignty of God. Here are a few:

GOD GOVERNS THE HEARTS OF KINGS AND ALL IN AUTHORITY.

> The king's heart is a stream of water in the hand of the Lord; He turns it wherever He will. (Proverbs 21:1; cf. Ezra 6:22)

GOD CONTROLS BOTH SIDES OF THE PROBLEM.

> The deceived and the deceiver are his. (Job 12:16)

GOD DESTROYS OR MODIFIES ANY PLAN HE WISHES.

> The LORD brings the counsel of the nations to nought; He frustrates the plans of the peoples. The counsel of the LORD stands forever, the thoughts of His heart to all generations. (Psalm 33:10-11)

GOD USES EVIL FOR HIS OWN PURPOSES.

> Who has commanded and it came to pass, unless the Lord has ordained it? Is it not from the mouth of the Most High that good and evil come? (Lamentations 3:37-38)

> Does evil befall a city, unless the Lord has done it? (Amos 3:6)

GOD CAUSES ALL THINGS TO WORK TOGETHER FOR GOOD—EVEN WHEN THEY ARE MEANT FOR EVIL.

> And Joseph said to his brothers, "Please come near to me." So they came near. Then he said: "I am Joseph your brother, whom you sold into Egypt. But now, do not

therefore be grieved or angry with yourselves because you sold me here; for God sent me before you to preserve life. For these two years the famine has been in the land, and there are still five years in which there will be neither plowing nor harvesting. And God sent me before you to preserve a posterity for you in the earth, and to save your lives by a great deliverance. So now it was not you who sent me here, but God; and He has made me a father to Pharaoh, and lord of all his house, and a ruler throughout all the land of Egypt." (Genesis 45:4-8)

Then his brothers also went and fell down before his face, and they said, "Behold, we are your servants." Joseph said to them, "Do not be afraid, for am I in the place of God? But as for you, you meant evil against me; but God meant it for good, in order to bring it about as it is this day, to save many people alive. Now therefore, do not be afraid; I will provide for you and your little ones." And he comforted them and spoke kindly to them. (Genesis 50:18-21)

GOD HARDENS THE HEARTS OF WHOMEVER HE PLEASES.

But Sihon king of Heshbon would not let us pass through, for the Lord your God hardened his spirit and made his heart obstinate, that He might deliver him into your hand, as it is this day.   (Deuteronomy 2:30)

GOD TESTS HIS PEOPLE WITH TRIALS.

And Moses said to the people, "Do not fear; for God has come to test you, and that His fear may be before you, so that you may not sin." (Exodus 20:20)

GOD RULES EVERYTHING.

In whose hand is the life of every living thing, and the breath of all mankind? Does not the ear test words and the mouth taste its food? Wisdom is with aged men, and with length of days, understanding. With Him are wisdom and strength, He has counsel and understanding. If He breaks a thing down, it cannot be rebuilt; If He imprisons a man, there can be no release. If He withholds the waters, they dry up; if He sends them out, they overwhelm the earth. With Him are strength and prudence. The deceived and the deceiver are His. He leads counselors away plundered, and makes fools of the judges. He loosens the bonds of kings, and binds their waist with a belt. He leads princes away plundered, and overthrows the mighty. He deprives the trusted ones of speech, and takes away the discernment of the elders. He pours contempt on princes, and disarms the mighty. He uncovers deep things out of darkness, and brings the shadow of death to light. He makes nations great, and destroys them; He enlarges nations, and guides them. He takes away the understanding of the chiefs of the people of the earth, and makes them wander in a pathless wilderness. They grope in the dark without light, And He makes them stagger like a drunken man. (Job 12:10-25)

These statements may not conform to a popular understanding of God, but they are what the Bible says of Him. This is where we must begin, for our vision of God is the foundation of our view of history, defines our lives, and affects every relationship we will ever have. Our denial or acknowledgement of God's sovereignty will either make us wring our hands in worry, or cause us to lift them up to heaven and say, "My times are in Your hands" (Psalm 31:15).

A Father Must

1. MAKE CLEAR THE TRUTH OF GOD'S SOVEREIGN POWER.

Fathers need to make several things clear to their sons as they prepare them to contemplate their lives:

First, the events of the past are not accidents.

Second, the events of the past are ordained by God for His glory.

Third, the events of the past will work together for His people's good.

The truth of Holy Scripture is that God will always give His children a way through whatever dire straits He ordains.

This understanding of history filled the heart of Joseph. After all the wrongs committed against him, he seemed completely absent of distress, anger, or bitterness from the difficulties he experienced. Joseph was trained as a youth with severe testing as a despised brother, a slave, and a prisoner (Genesis 37-50). He was wrongly accused by the promiscuous wife of his master and then left to rot in prison. But, he didn't rot his youth away in prison. Instead, he became the caretaker of the prison - the direct result of his lifestyle of faithfulness. He spent his entire youth, from age seventeen to age thirty-two, either as a slave or a prisoner. And when he looked back upon it all, he saw the mighty hand of God at work. Joseph knew and obeyed a big God, the one who controls everything. This providential view of history implanted within him a fearlessness that was the secret of his usefulness. He was not frightened by any fear, because he saw the hand of God moving in history.

Fathers, don't let your sons leave home without bearing in hand and heart the doctrine of the sovereignty of God. Say to them, "Do not be terrified; do not be discouraged!"

> Have I not commanded you? Be strong and of good courage; do not be afraid, nor be dismayed, for the Lord your God is with you wherever you go. (Joshua 1:9)

"Son, Trust in the Sovereign Hand of God"

EVERY SON NEEDS TO HEAR
HIS FATHER SAY:

"Son, Accept Tough Discipline in Training"

For consider Him who endured such hostility from sinners against Himself, lest you become weary and discouraged in your souls. You have not yet resisted to bloodshed, striving against sin. And you have forgotten the exhortation which speaks to you as sons: "My son, do not despise the chastening of the Lord, nor be discouraged when you are rebuked by Him; for whom the Lord loves He chastens. And scourges every son whom He receives."

- Hebrews 12:3-6

CHAPTER 9

TRAINING HARDER THAN THE REAL THING

If a father understands up front what his training principles will be, he will do a better job of preparing his son for action. All my life I heard my father's maxim, "The training should be harder than the real thing." He repeated this statement to our family dozens of times as we were growing up, when referring to some taxing moment we were experiencing.

My dad's survival as a pilot depended on the fact that, wherever possible, the training was harder than the real thing would be. The cumulative experiences of planned hardship and testing in training prepared him for the moments ahead where in a flash he would have to respond the right way or be killed. Training that is harder than the real thing has a way of refining the intuitive and instantaneous reactions. This is the stuff of survival. This is the backdrop of "mission accomplished."

A wide range of experiences and disciplines made up my father's training to be a pilot. There were hardships, joys, and disappointments, all adding up to the training that helped keep him alive during World War II.

I have heard many stories about his training to be a WWII pilot. Here are a few things he experienced during his training:

- Opportunity
- Fear
- Privilege
- Exhaustion
- Danger
- Stupid mistakes
- Mentors—good and bad
- Competition
- Disasters
- Recoveries
- Embarrassment
- Exposure
- Failure
- Camaraderie
- Sickness
- Risk
- Competence
- Laughter

There is no shortcut to success. Rather, it is forged during hours and hours of arduous, repetitive, exhausting training.

As noted in earlier chapters, it is recognized there are times when it is impossible to match any training to the savagery that takes place in the true battle. However, the purpose of training is to prepare diligently and wholeheartedly for the worst case we can antici-pate. To create prepared and appropriate reactions to as many situations we can imagine and trust God to make up the difference as he determines in His wisdom.

Sons need to know that there are dangerous pitfalls that can keep them from the full value of their training.

A Father Must

1. DISCUSS FEAR.

Fear of failure or embarrassment, sickness, hardship or exhaustion can ruin the effectiveness of your training, yielding a self-perpetuating poor attitude and sucking the value out of the experience. Fear of failure is usually a form of self-love causing us to look for an inexpensive, easy, painless, trouble-free training experience. We instinctively shrink away from true training; the multi-year experiences which require repetition and, more often than not, two steps forward and one step back.

This is important for both fathers and sons to grasp. They may be tempted to throw up their hands and say, "This is too much of a hassle." Remember the words of the wise, "The best colts need breaking in."

2. . BE COMPASSIONATE IN TRUTH.

Some fathers equate compassion with taking the easy road through life and causing as little pain as possible. Fathers must be willing to take their children through some of the pain that is associated with discipline. Fathers must know that their job is NOT to constantly please their children by approving all of their own inclinations. On the one hand, fathers must focus their activities on what their sons are gifted or able to do, and on the other hand, they must expand their experiences beyond their sons' own inclina-tions. There are times when the training should be very difficult for children to endure. A good father will be committed to making his children come to grips with greater things than the children can conceive in their own minds. Of course, there is always the danger of exasperating children, but these dangers do not erase the responsibility to discipline.

Fathers have a responsibility to provide training that is harder than the real thing—and sometimes harder than children desire. I am sure that the biblical character Joseph understood this (Genesis 37-50). He was buffeted by years of rejection and imprisonment and slavery in his preparation to rule. The training was hard, but God had something in mind for which Joseph could never have prepared on his own—only hard training could have prepared him.

Fathers who train this way will be able to train up their children in the discipline and admonition of the Lord. In the process, they will not be afraid to discipline them, teach them, correct them, and encourage them...remembering that the training often needs to be harder than the real thing.

"Son, Accept Tough Discipline in Training"

EVERY SON NEEDS TO HEAR
HIS FATHER SAY:

"Son, Consider It Joy When You Encounter Trials"

I will show him what great things he must
suffer for my name's sake

- Acts 9:16

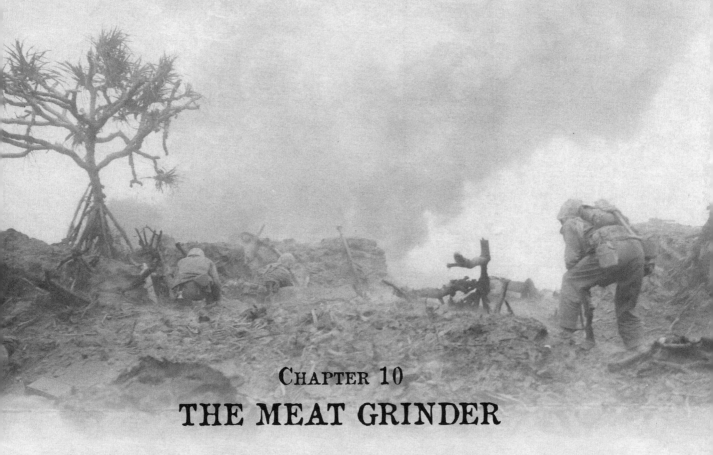

CHAPTER 10
THE MEAT GRINDER

My father used the term "The Meat Grinder" many times during my childhood. I never really knew the origin of the term, except from the context in which he used it. I knew it meant a place where people get torn up. So I grew up with the consciousness that there were situations—meat grinders—in life which are harsh situations. These shaking circumstances are often tests of faith which either make us or break us.

Many years later, I would learn that The Meat Grinder was the location of one of the most horrible battles on Iwo Jima where an entire Marine company was closed down. Deep within my father's memories are images of flamethrowers, walls of artillery fire, grenades, and an impenetrable wall of resistance called Hill 382. This famous Iwo Jima battle exhausted and extinguished the lives of many—500 died the first day of battle.

This place was actually known by a number of other terms besides "The

Meat Grinder": "Turkey Knob," "The Amphitheater," and "Hill 382" were a few.

It was a harmless-looking hill, only 382 feet above sea level. Hence the name, "Hill 382."

It was the second-highest point on Iwo Jima, giving a 360-degree view of the island. The Japanese possession of this location gave them the ability to see everything going on from the base of Mount Suribachi all the way to the extreme north end of Iwo Jima.

The Marines took this hill six times and lost it five times.[1]

This is from the combat record from the battle:

> FROM 1800, 26 FEB 45 TO 1800, 27 FEB 45 (D PLUS 8)
>
> Hill 382, one of the most vital terrain features in this area, was made up of a series of deep fissures or crevices which blended well into the scheme of the Japanese defense. It was envisaged that the capture of this terrain-freak would be a costly and a time-consuming job.[2]

My father remembers watching a flamethrower tank a hundred yards away from him taking out a pillbox on "The Meat Grinder." He saw men black with blood and grime and smoke staggering back from the battle line and collapsing, completely spent from several days there.

That hill was the nerve center of the enemy's defenses for the north end. Like Suribachi, it was a complex system of caves and pillboxes with tunnels running through it. A cross-section of the hill makes you think of an ant farm and its tunnels and passageways. There were at least three levels. One cave

ran eight hundred yards to a nearby "village" while another had fourteen entrances.

The gallantry that characterized the victory at "The Meat Grinder" is exemplified in the Medal of Honor recipient Private First Class Douglas T. Jacobson. The congressional record reads:

> [Private Jacobson] destroyed a total of sixteen enemy positions and annihilated approximately seventy-five Japanese, thereby contributing essentially to the success of his division's operations against the fanatically defended outpost of the Japanese Empire. His gallant conduct in the face of tremendous odds enhanced and sustained the highest traditions of the United States Naval Service.[3]

The "Meat Grinder" was a trial of Gargantuan proportions. Welcome to life on Iwo.

Trials are a part of life and courage must be there to meet them. Courage is something that fathers can promote in their sons by helping them understand some of the fine points about suffering. If they know what they are facing, they will better be able to handle it.

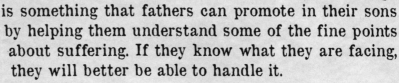

113

A Father Must

1. TEACH OF SURPRISES AND DRAMATIC CHANGES IN LIFE.

Often some of the most innocent and safe-looking situations become meat grinders for us. We are going along in life and then there is a trial of magnificent proportions that emerges from one "harmless" situation. In the journey of life, hills that seem to be small at first sight may become high mountains where you might become sick, destitute, or rejected by friends and family. Some of the changes that happen to us at these times may be permanent.

Hill 382 looked safe enough upon approach. But as Captain Ridlon said, "You barely know it's there. But when we climbed it, it was higher than anything I ever saw."[4]

It was at "The Meat Grinder" that E Company (Easy Company) fought. This was the outfit which raised the flag on Mount Suribachi. But "The Meat Grinder" would wipe them out forever. After eight days of battle, the casualties would be so heavy that they would mean the end of E Company. The day after the battle ended, the weary remnants of E Company would be reassigned to F Company.

2. SHOW THAT SOMETIMES SUFFERING IS THE ONLY WAY TO VICTORY.

The battle for Iwo Jima could not be won without taking Hill 382. It was a necessary sacrifice, for it put victory within view, but it came at a high price. The Meat Grinder teaches us that war is a parable of hardship and loss. It exposes us to times of pressure and loss that may be necessary to accomplish a greater goal.

3. NEVER BE DISMAYED.

There are times when we must go through a meat grinder to get to the final victory. The meat grinders of life take on many forms—a natural disaster, the loss of a child, a financial cataclysm, a broken relationship, or a family problem. Our loving God, who desires to refine us like fire to make us into His own image designs all of the challenges we face. We can persevere, because we know that God is doing something in our lives and the current trial is His tool.

My brethren, count it all joy when you fall into various trials, knowing that the testing of your faith produces patience. But let patience have its perfect work, that you may be perfect and complete, lacking nothing. (James 1:2-3)

For the time would fail me to tell of Gideon and Barak and Samson and Jephthah, also of David and Samuel and the prophets: who through faith subdued kingdoms, worked righteousness, obtained promises, stopped the mouths of lions, quenched the violence of fire, escaped the edge of the sword, out of weakness were made strong, became valiant in battle, turned to flight the armies of the aliens. Women received their dead raised to life again. And others were tortured, not accepting deliverance, that they might obtain a better resurrection. Still others had trial of mockings and scourgings, yes, and of chains and imprisonment. They were stoned, they were sawn in two, were tempted, were slain with the sword. They wandered about in sheepskins and goatskins, being destitute, afflicted, tormented—of whom the world was not worthy. They wandered in deserts and mountains, in dens and caves of the earth. And all these, having obtained a good testimony through faith, did not receive the promise, God having provided something better for us, that they should not be made perfect apart from us. (Hebrews 11:32-40)

...that no one should be shaken by these afflictions; for you yourselves know that we are appointed to this. (I Thessalonians 3:3)

"Son, Consider It Joy When You Encounter Trials"

EVERY SON NEEDS TO HEAR
HIS FATHER SAY:
"Son, Don't Pre-judge Disasters"

My times are in Your hand.

- Psalm 31:15

Chapter 11
BLACK FRIDAY

Pre-judging disasters is something boys should learn to avoid. When difficult circumstances strike, our tendency is to over-interpret them, and we often come to wrong conclusions and become subject to the wrong feelings they generate. This can lead one to all manner of misinterpretation, which can further cause him to mislead himself as well as others. The reality is that the presumptuous often experience significant angst at the beginning, but are often later pleasantly surprised that the disaster turned out to be the gateway for the blessings of the Lord.

The worst Pacific War disaster of the Seventh Air Force happened on June 1, 1945, when twenty-five P-51 Mustangs from the 15th Fighter Group took off from Iwo Jima and twenty-four of them never came back. Twenty-three of the twenty-five pilots were killed. No one knows exactly why this happened. The most likely culprit was Typhoon Nana. It was probable that a powerful wind from the typhoon caught twenty-three pilots by surprise.

The storm took their flying formation and mangled them together sending them to their deaths.

Their calamity came as they were on a massive bombing offensive against Osaka with all three fighter commands in the air—170 Mustangs on escort. 250 miles from Iwo Jima this gigantic force passed over the leading edge of clouds that reached over the horizon. They assumed that the storm had been properly analyzed and judged safe. The communication was unclear, and in the wake of the tragedy there were heated accusations and debates among the Air Corps brass.

Only two men from the 15th Fighter Group came back from that mission. They were my father's friends and fellow squadron pilots, Eddie Bates and Second Lieutenant Arthur Burry. Both came home from the war and lived long lives. I had the pleasure of getting to know them when they were in their eighties.

While the other 23 planes were lost in the midst of the gigantic storm, Eddie and Art were the only survivors of that mission—because of engine trouble. If their engines had performed well, they most likely would have been thrown to their deaths with the other men.

Eddie Bates' plane was malfunctioning so he broke away from the group and headed back to Iwo before everything came unglued. He made it back safely without any further mishaps.

Arthur Burry's airplane started malfunctioning also, so he pulled away from the group and headed back toward Iwo Jima alone. Unfortunately, Burry's engine quit about half-way between Japan and Iwo.

He was flying the P51 he had dubed the "Betty Ellen." Burry was engaged to a girl named Betty back home. The other fellow who flew the plane was married to Ellen. Hence the name of the plane,

"Betty Ellen."

When Arthur Burry realized that "Betty Ellen" was destined for the bottom of the Pacific Ocean, he made preparations to bail out. At about 2,000 feet, he crawled out of the cockpit and down the side to the wing and slipped off into the air—missing the tail, as other pilots were sometimes not so fortunate to do.

His parachute opened, and if he had any illusions that he was floating to safety, they were dashed soon enough. He was dropping into a section of the Pacific Ocean that was about to be hammered by a massive typhoon—Typhoon Nana. The congressional record would contain these words:

His survival is one of the miracles of this war.

It was fairly calm when he plunged into the Pacific Ocean that day, but the weather was turning fast. In his one-man rubber raft, Arthur Burry would soon be riding fifty-foot waves and be blasted by winds in excess of one hundred miles per hour—and he was 275 miles from the mainland of Japan in a raft not much bigger than the lower half of his body.

For the entire six days he spent in the raft, he would drink only about half a quart of water and eat a handful of pemmican. This privation would nearly kill him.

Typhoons strike fear into the hearts of all seafarers who have ever had to ride them out. Each year they roll through the Pacific islands causing all to remember how small we are in the midst of powers that can be absolutely devastating.

While Burry was bobbing in the fifty-foot waves in his one-man rubber raft, Typhoon Nana was wrecking some of the largest ships in Admiral Halsey's fleet:

The heavy cruiser USS Pittsburgh (CA-72) lost its bow, and two other cruisers suffered frame damage.

Several aircraft carriers sustained flight deck damage.

The USS Belleau Wood (LHA-3) had her elevator destroyed.

The destroyer USS Samuel N. Moore (DD-747) suffered major super-structure damage.

Escort carriers USS Windham Bay (CVE-92) and USS Salamaua (CVE-96) had part of their flight decks blown off.

The tanker USS Millicoma (AO-73) suffered substantial topside damage.

Furthermore, Nana destroyed forty-three planes and swept thrity-three overboard.[1]

The contrasts are stark...while these large ships were getting their decks ripped off, their bows broken in half and their frames mangled, Arthur Burry was bobbing in his little rubber life raft.

In training, my dad and Burry were taught to tie themselves to their rafts. To do this, you had to save some of the parachute shroud line before letting the chute go. The chute must be released or it will drag you all over the ocean. Fortunately, Burry tied himself to the raft, keeping the raft close by as the waves crashed over him again and again.

The congressional record reads:

Pacific Fleet Headquarters, Guam—Forced down in Japanese waters, a Mustang fighter pilot, Second Lt. Arthur A. Burry of Davenport, Iowa, rode out the full fury of a typhoon in his frail one man rubber raft. His survival is one of the miracles of this war...Burry, a husky lad of 21 had been on this tiny, bobbing raft...For hours as the typhoon howled with unabated force, he clung desperately to his raft. Several times—he doesn't remember how many—he was washed off by the impact of the towering waves, which swallowed his craft bouncing him around like a rubber ball. But each time Burry managed to crawl back aboard. How, he does not know.[2]

One day a sea gull landed on the raft but Burry was afraid to shoot it with his 45, because he thought he might hit his foot.

Near the end of the six days, he was incoherently babbling about his impending rescue by his flyer comrades. He knew those comrades would come; he could hear them overhead. He called out to them and he could hear them. They were just over the horizon now, and he could hear them laughing and talking and singing. They seemed to be having a party. "I knew I could hear them just as plainly as I hear you," young Burry insisted stoutly to his rescuers later. "They seemed to be having a good time, and I remember I got mad because they didn't invite me to the party. But I was never really worried; I knew the boys would come and take me out of there." Hosking said that Burry's body was covered with sores. His skin was badly lacerated, apparently from constant rubbing against the rubber fabric of the raft. He also was extremely sunburned. He was delirious.

DAY ONE: He landed in the water at 1100. Later in the day he saw B-29s returning from strike and used five tracers, one die marker, and one star flare to attract their attention.

DAY TWO: Weather closed in to the deck. The water was a little choppy.

DAY THREE: Lt. Burry saw B-29s en route to Japan, so he put out a day marker and sent up one flare which was not seen. He ate nothing and drank a little more water.

DAY FOUR: It started raining. He did not catch any water as he had used only a half can of water so far. He ate one-fourth can of pemmican. He put up the sail, "just for something to do." After an hour, he took it down.

DAY FIVE: The typhoon strength increased and waves dumped him five times. He had tied the backpack to the handle of the raft but it became untied and he lost it, losing his food.

DAY SIX: The sun came out and it was calm except for the big swells. He began to have delusions. He was at a party on the ocean in a barn with other pilots from his squadron. He kept asking for a drink and his friends would offer him one. As he grabbed for it the drink would vanish. At the party he met a friend of a friend who said he worked in the control tower and promised to send a destroyer for him.

DAY SEVEN: He started hearing music, and distant voices of people singing songs. As he heard the music he started to whistle and call to attract attention of the singers. He distinctly heard voices of other men in his squadron, including my father's voice. [3]

Soon the voices grew louder and louder, closer and closer.

Then the submarine Trutta appeared while on rescue duty. Rescue duty meant that the sub would leave Guam, pass by Iwo, and head toward Japan looking for downed flyers. The Trutta was seeking refuge from the storm by going deep to escape the turbulent waters above. Usually it was calm at two hundred feet, but not on this day; it was unusually rough and murky, tossing the submarine around, even at the depth of two hundred feet, all because of Nana. The Trutta decided to come up to see if it might be better on the surface. Even though the waves were still at fifty feet, the captain ordered two men to get up in the conning tower to look for downed airmen with their binoculars. It just so happened that at the same time the submarine was on the crest of a fifty-foot wave, Burry's raft was on the crest of another wave, at just the right moment for the men to see it. The sub immediately started for the place they last saw the rubber raft.

When men from the Trutta first approached his raft and threw him a rope, Burry threw it back and told them that his men were sending a destroyer for him. He did this twice, so the third time they just grabbed him. He was picked up 300 miles north of Iwo on a direct line to Osaka. The Trutta crew members welcomed him in the sub, gaining another family member, forming a bond between him and the crew not to be broken in the coming decades of his life.

The Trutta never sank any ships or found herself in the right place at the right time for heroism. Burry's rescue may have been one of the most important things the crew members did during the war, and they celebrate it every year—The Rescue of Arthur Burry.

This should not be forgotten. It speaks so clearly of the miracle-working

hand of God in time of storm. The odds of survival were almost nil, but God had a different plan for Burry.

No matter how bad it gets, there are greater powers at work and God is the governor of those powers. He will, by the force of His own perfect and unstoppable will, bring glory to Himself even when things look the darkest.

Not only did the Trutta save Arthur Burry's life, but a newspaper clipping about the incident, would have a remarkable effect...years later.

Immediately after Arthur Burry was rescued by the submarine Trutta, the Davenport, Iowa Democrat newspaper ran a story on the rescue. The front page headline read:

Davenporter, Adrift at Sea Six Days Off Japan, Tells of His Struggle to Survive

The article contained a picture of Arthur Burry as well as a detailed story of his experience in the typhoon. This newspaper clipping would start a chain of events that would reunite Burry with his long-lost family.

When Burry was a boy of two and a half years old, his mother died in an automobile accident and the family fell on hard times. His father was not able to provide for his family so, under the advice of friends and counsel of professionals, he determined that the best thing for the children was to put all eight of them into an orphanage. So, the eight children, from nine months to sixteen years old, were placed in an orphanage in Davenport, Iowa. A year later, Arthur (age three) and his two youngest sisters left the orphanage, adopted into good homes. The remaining five children stayed in the orphanage until they graduated from high school and then moved to different places around the country.

In the spring of 1948, two years after the end of the war, one of Arthur's long-lost sisters, who was thirty-two years old at the time, was cleaning out her attic. She picked up a stack of old newspapers, took it to the trash, and went back upstairs to get another load. Back in the attic, she looked down and saw the picture on the front page of the Davenport Democrat.

The article was about a pilot's rescue by a submarine during the war. She looked at the picture and thought to herself, "That officer looks a lot like my brother Hank. I wonder if that could be my long lost brother Arther." Hank was one of her other brothers whom she had seen in uniform. She thought that the man in the newspaper looked enough like Hank to find out if it was indeed Arthur. She quickly contacted the newspaper to see if there were any leads. After following up on those contacts, she learned that the other family members had moved out of town. Continuing to follow the leads, she found Arthur's address and sent a letter to him in Los Angeles saying that she wondered if he could be her brother. She was right...the rescued pilot in the Democrat story was her younger brother. She gave him contact information for some of the other siblings, and through these connections, the family was reunited. This was the unintended consequence of the failure of Burry's plane and six days riding out the worst typhoon of the Pacific War.

The kind providences of God often come in the form of some "failure" or "disaster" that sends us on an altogether different course than the one on which we were traveling. In this case, engine failures saved two men's lives and started the series of events that would bring long scattered siblings together. Stories like these remind us that we should reserve judgment about our trials and tribulations for another time. God knows what He is doing through all our sufferings.

Burry's six days at sea in a one-man raft is a good example of how blessings are often cleverly disguised as difficulties.

Often we interpret events wrongly by prematurely declaring them disasters. Later on we see that God was working a better plan. He orders our steps so that His glory will be revealed—even when we think we are in a time of disaster.

Now as Jesus passed by, He saw a man who was blind from birth. And His disciples asked Him, saying, "Rabbi, who sinned, this man or his parents, that he was born blind?" Jesus answered, "Neither this man nor his parents sinned, but that the works of God should be revealed in him." (John 9:1-3)

A Father Must

1. RECOGNIZE AND TEACH THAT GOD'S PLANS ARE THE BEST PLANS.

A father must not be overly presumptuous himself. He may be tempted to weigh in on a matter that he should leave to the judgment of God. That judgment may or may not come in this lifetime for God is working across a wide range of lives and circumstances and some things need to be left in the hands of God to discern. Presuming to know "why" is a study in futility.

> Surely oppression destroys a wise man's reason, and a bribe debases the heart. The end of a thing is better than its beginning; the patient in spirit is better than the proud in spirit. Do not hasten in your spirit to be angry, for anger rests in the bosom of fools. Do not say, "Why were the former days better than these?" For you do not inquire wisely concerning this. (Ecclesiastes 7:7-10)

Sixty years after the end of the war, I asked Lt. Burry, "What is the lesson from the life raft?" He quickly replied, "Be thankful." He says that he was always thankful to be rescued, but when his engine quite, he never dreamed just how thankful he would be for all the things that happened as a result of that famous typhoon and that submarine rescue.

> He sent from above, He took me; He drew me out of many waters. He delivered me from my strong enemy, from those who hated me, for they were too strong for me. They confronted me in the day of my calamity, but the Lord was my support. He also brought me out into a broad place; He delivered me because He delighted in me. (Psalm 18:16-19)

"Son, Don't Pre-judge Disasters"

EVERY SON NEEDS TO HEAR
HIS FATHER SAY:
"Son, The Lord Goes Before You"

And it shall be, when you hear a sound of marching...then you shall go out to battle, for God has gone out before you.

- 1 Chronicles 14:15

Chapter 12
SHOT DOWN IN ENEMY WATERS

Since I was a little boy, my father told me about the day he was shot down over enemy waters during a raid on Yokohama. The story tugs at me because it details one of the most powerful aspects of fatherhood. This was displayed in the words my grandfather spoke to my dad the day he left for the Pacific.

On that day, Grandpa Brown drove to the military base and presented his son with a pocket Bible. This was a very special moment for my grandfather, because, as a pastor, he had already performed numerous funerals for the families of boys who had died in the war. As he handed it to him he said, "Son, the Lord goes before you." The memory of those words would come back to the son repeatedly in the days ahead.

The next time my father saw his dad was 1945 - the end of the war.

My father never forgot those words. Now over a half a century later, he still repeats them to me. Here is a son (my father) who heard six words out of the mouth of his father (my grandfather), and these words were so precious to him that he has recited them his whole life long. My grandfather's words were powerful for a reason. They were strongly reminiscent of the words of God to King David as he was preparing for battle, "And it shall be, when you hear a sound of marching...then you shall go out to battle, for God has gone out before you..." (1 Chronicles 14:15).

These words carried my dad through the most harrowing experiences of his life and they have lived on in him and then multiplied into the hearts of others.

My dad arrived on Iwo Jima on D+8, or February 26, 1945. His Airfield, #1 (the one closest to Suribachi), had just barely been secured and was still under Japanese mortar fire while it was being repaired.

Upon arrival, he hit the beach and walked about a mile to dig a foxhole with a shovel just like the one he gave me when I was a boy. He dug his foxhole three feet deep and lived there for ten or twelve days until the flight surgeons ordered the pilots be put into tents because of excessive sickness.

Even so, he maintained a posture of fearlessness, and remembered, "Son, the Lord goes before you." He could easily say along with the Psalmist, "When the wicked came against me to eat up my flesh, my enemies and foes, they stumbled and fell. Though an army may encamp against me, my heart shall not fear. Though war may rise against me, in this I will be confident" (Psalm 27:1-3).

The clamor of war was always in the air and conditions were difficult. Temperatures in February and March were cold at night, 45 degrees, while the daytime climate was hot and muggy and the conditions on every level were destabilizing.

Dad carried a Colt 45 plastic-handled pistol in a shoulder holster and tracer bullets in the magazine for night fire. This way he could see where he was firing and could, if needed, use his gun as a rescue device. He also carried a compass, a shovel, a can of water, a can of pemmican (terrible), and the best Hershey bar ever made (three inches long and one inch thick).

He was issued two flight suits with pockets all over them, and he wore a soft Air Force hat with a wool liner because he did not like the uncomfortable steel hat. In the pockets he carried orange flares—another reminder of the vulnerability of his position.

During the daytime my dad would go to the airfield to see how things were progressing, waiting for the planes to arrive. While killing time, he got to know an "old" Seabee—thirty-five years of age—who would let Dad use his bulldozer to push dirt into holes because he was preparing airfields and covering up Japanese cave openings.

The Mustangs finally arrived March 7. The Army Air Corps was in the air the next day as ground support for a battle on the north end. Then came other assignments—flying interdiction missions against Japanese aerial attacks and raiding nearby targets like Chi Chi Jima.

Life on Iwo Jima was as threatening as it was grimy, but there were some unexpected bright spots. For instance, Gene Autry came to Iwo in the middle of March. Shooting was still going on and you could hear both American and Japanese gunfire during the show. After the show, Mr. Autry had supper with Dad's squadron of forty-six guys. Autry's famous cowboy hat was a perfect fit for Dad, so he wore it for an hour while Autry put on another show for five hundred men. He sang some of my favorite cowboy songs like "Back in the Saddle Again" and "Git Along Little Dogies." We have a picture of Dad in that hat.

My dad says that because there was so much death on Iwo, they quit having funerals. The chaplains felt that the constant funerals would have a negative effect on the men, so the ceremonies were suspended.

One day, my father was the last one left alive in his tent:

> Three of the four of us in the tent had been killed. The flight surgeon did not want to leave me alone in a tent, so he moved me to another tent that had some other pilots in it. We were at a psychological point that when people were lost, it seemed normal. Death was normal. We didn't develop deep friendships except for maybe one person. But this I remembered, "Son, the Lord goes before you."

I have always been struck by the casual and disarming way my father faced war and death. It was almost as if he was not aware of the dangers. He seemed to think that none of the bullets had his name on them and he never for a moment thought that he would die in combat. This attitude persisted even in spite of the fact that every day there were other flyboys who never came back from their missions.

He says he was enabled to maintain this attitude because of his father's parting words and the atmosphere that filled his home life every day of his youth. Back home the words of the great hymns of the faith wafted through the house as his faithful mother would sing them over and over again. This was her way of making their home a haven of peace. She never had a driver's license and kept her entire focus on making her home the most wonderful place in the world. She would sing "Blessed Assurance," "Blest Be the Tie that Binds," "Wonderful Words of Life," and "The Old Rugged Cross." In addition to this, Dad's father was a Methodist pastor, and he grew up daily hearing the words of Scripture coming from his father's mouth daily.

Looking back on those days my dad said,

> My worldview was that I was being directed and protected. Every day our leaders were leading us into "the valley of the shadow of death." But in my heart I sang, "Faith of our fathers, living still" and "The Lord goes before you."

My dad was calm in the midst of battle because he believed that the Lord went before him and that he was being held in everlasting arms. He believed that "He [God] is a shield to all who trust in Him" (Psalm 18:30). It was his vision of God that sustained him, even when he was the only one left in his tent. All around him there was evidence that his demise was imminent, but the knowledge of God overwhelmed the power of the evidence that dogged him every day. This is the only secure source of true confidence and fearlessness.

Dad flew eighteen sorties during his service on Iwo Jima, but on May 29 he flew his last. On that day, he was launched on one of the largest air assaults against Japan. My father was flying one of the 101 P-51 Mustangs escorting four hundred B-29s to the target—Yokahoma, the mainland of Japan.

One of the largest Japanese fighter forces ever assembled came out to meet them. Yokahoma was a city of 900,000 population. On that day "47% of it was destroyed in a single attack lasting less than an hour."[1]

My father was in one of the only two Mustangs lost that day. The pilot of the other Mustang was not so fortunate. While trying to chase off a Zeke, Lieutenant Rufus Moore's plane was heavily damaged and he plunged into the ocean. My dad's plane was hit, but by God's grace he bailed out and lived to tell about it.

It was a picture-perfect day. The skies were blue and the sea was green. Mount Fuji stood out beautifully against the horizon from the island of Japan. He could see the bombers as his plane climbed up and prepared to cover them.

Without warning, a Zero appeared dead ahead. Dad and his flight leader were shooting at the enemy. All of a sudden, there was no sound—his engine had stopped. In the midst of the turmoil, my dad's plane was hit and he took a tracer bullet in his neck. His flight leader disappeared in the sky somewhere, and as he looked around he couldn't see the Zero anywhere. So he pushed over and built up a lot of speed.

He got his engine started again and started south toward Tokyo Bay. A few minutes later, he saw a group of B-29s who had already left the target and were heading south again. He stayed far away from them, flying parallel with them for a while. Then he eased in a little closer.

All of a sudden, he looked down and saw that he didn't have functioning instruments any more. He looked out on the wing and saw that the gasoline caps had popped off and were smoking. A pilots worst nightmare. his plane was on fire.

He had been shot by "friendly fire." He said, "When you are in combat, you are excited. When you see something and you really can't identify it, you shoot at it. When you are excited, sometimes you shoot first and ask questions later." The B-29 had a very good firing system for that time, his crippled, burning plane was proof of that.

In training he and his fellow pilots had watched movies on how to get out of an airplane. When you are in a crippled plane, you have to trust your parachute. So he rolled the plane upside-down and tried to fall out, just the way his C.O. had said.

He followed procedure, but it didn't work, he could not fall out, so—plan "B"—he rolled it back and quickly crawled out on the right side, having already dumped the fiberglass canopy.

Miraculously, his chute worked. Just a month before, they had taken a dozen chutes from his squadron, put sandbags on them, and dumped them off over the field; half of those parachutes didn't open.

Reflecting on this my dad said, "When you are in combat, as well as when you are flying in the training command, you have an attitude that your plane is going to fly and your equipment will work well and that the Lord is with you. Even in desperate situations like this one just south of Tokyo Bay, I knew the Lord went before me and that He would spare me at His pleasure—so there was nothing to fear."

He was at about eight thousand feet when his parachute billowed. He dropped through light cumulus clouds and on down to the water. He was able to see a little Japanese island (it could have been Oshima) over a few miles to the side. Then, there was that unforgettable moment when he saw the little circle in the ocean that his plane made when it went "whoosh"

into the Pacific. When he got in the water it was just like in the movies—
"Nothing to it."

Dad said, "They had trained us in Richmond, Virginia, in a swimming pool. They had shown us some movies on how to do this. We had a sergeant who showed us over and over and over again how to get in and out of a one-man life raft. It was a piece of cake. I got into that raft and had to decide whether I was too close to that Japanese island to mess around with a smoke bomb signal."

Once in the water, he let go of two of his smoke bombs and waited a while—maybe ten or fifteen minutes. Then he let the rest of them go. There he was floating in his rubber raft wearing a life preserver, with only a bottle of water, Hershey bars, and two pills to calm him down, but when he hit the water, the pills, in his open pocket, and just dissolved away.

Before he knew it, a submarine surfaced next to him—the Pipefish. They must have seen him go down, or a bomber saw him and called in. He found out later that the Pipefish picked up nine flyers during its stint there in the Pacific.

After being picked up, he wasn't allowed to get off at Iwo, but was taken on to a sub base in Guam. He was debriefed, and the Red Cross sent a telegram to his parents in Pine Bluff, Arkansas. Three weeks before, in June of 1945, they had already received a War Department telegram saying that their son had been killed in action. His father had continued to preach. His mother continued to pray. Three weeks later they received the telegram that he had been picked up and was alive and well.

It is amazing how one story can symbolize whole worlds of knowledge. In this one event I have a reference point for the geography of the Pacific islands, the political climate in Japan during the war, the strategic nature of Iwo Jima, a cultural understanding of the "boys" who fought the Second World War, the importance of an air force in wartime, the planes of fame that ended the war, the radical courage that was necessary to overtake the most difficult island stronghold in the history of warfare, the personalities and the songs and the heartbreak of an entire era in U.S. history. However, the most important part of this story for me is summarized by the words my grandfather spoke to my father:

"SON, THE LORD GOES BEFORE YOU."

Surely the words of Psalm 139:3-6 were fulfilled that day he was shot down,

> You know my sitting down and my rising up; You understand my thought afar off. You comprehend my path and my lying down, and are acquainted with all my ways. For there is not a word on my tongue, but behold, O Lord, You know it altogether. You have hedged me behind and before, and laid Your hand upon me. Such knowledge is too wonderful for me.

The simple words of his father came back to strengthen him time after time. This was the secret of the attitude of my easy-going dad and the demeanor he possessed in one of the most dangerous places on earth. It is an example of how he handled things his whole life. He could always go through the most difficult situations with confidence and dignity because he knew that the Lord had already gone before him. Every day of his life he was always "Comin' in on a wing and a prayer." Ringing in his ears were the words he had heard all his life:

> God is our refuge and strength, a very present help in trouble. Therefore we will not fear, even though the earth be removed, and though the mountains be carried into the midst of the sea; though its waters roar and be troubled, though the mountains shake with its swelling. Selah. There is a river whose streams shall make glad the city of God, the holy place of the tabernacle of the Most High. God is in the midst of her, she shall not be moved; God shall help her, just at the break of dawn. The nations raged, the kingdoms were moved; He uttered His voice, the earth melted. The Lord of hosts is with us; the God of Jacob is our refuge. Selah! Come, behold the works of the Lord, who has made desolations in the earth. He makes wars

cease to the end of the earth; He breaks the bow and cuts the spear in two; He burns the chariot in the fire. Be still, and know that I am God; I will be exalted among the nations, I will be exalted in the earth! The Lord of hosts is with us; the God of Jacob is our refuge. Selah. (Psalm 46)

The words of my grandfather, which had such an impact on his son, continue to ring in my ears as well. My grandfather said "Son, the Lord goes before you" to his son. My father says to me "Son, the Lord goes before you." Now I am saying the same thing to my own son, the same thing that our Father in heaven has said to His sons for so many generations. The message is loud and clear and it has implications for all the days of my life. God seems to delight in appearing to his sons and saying, "Fear not...the Lord goes before you." He appeared to Jacob and said, "I am the God of your father Abraham; do not fear, for I am with you. I will bless you and multiply your descendants for My servant Abraham's sake" (Genesis 26:24).

In the same way that our Father in heaven tells us "Fear not, for I am with you," so we should tell our sons, "Son, the Lord goes before you." Pray that it rings in their ears all the days of their lives.

"Son, The Lord Goes Before You"

EVERY SON NEEDS TO HEAR
HIS FATHER SAY:

"Son, Sacrifice for the Next Generation"

You shall love the Lord your God with all your heart, with all your soul, and with all your strength. "And these words which I command you today shall be in your heart. You shall teach them diligently to your children, and shall talk of them when you sit in your house, when you walk by the way, when you lie down, and when you rise up."

- Deuteronomy 6:5-7

Chapter 13
FOR YOUR TOMORROW
WE GAVE OUR TODAY

Teaching boys the crux of biblical manhood is difficult today, because fallen cultures hold out such distorted pictures. Either you get a model of unhealthy domination or frail passivity. Yet, there is a scene from the battle of Iwo Jima that points to the heart of biblical manhood. The most prominent feature of biblical manhood is self-sacrifice. "The Son of Man did not come to be served, but to serve, and to give His life a ransom for many" (Matthew 20:28). "Husbands, love your wives as Christ loved the church and gave Himself for her" (Ephesians 5:22-33). Sadly, uninformed, biblically ignorant people assert that the Bible teaches some form of selfish male domination. On the contrary, the biblical teaching on male headship is demonstrably sacrificial and full of mercy.

Bill Henderson went ashore with the Fifth Marine Division. On that day, the Fourth and Fifth Marine Divisions put almost forty thousand men on

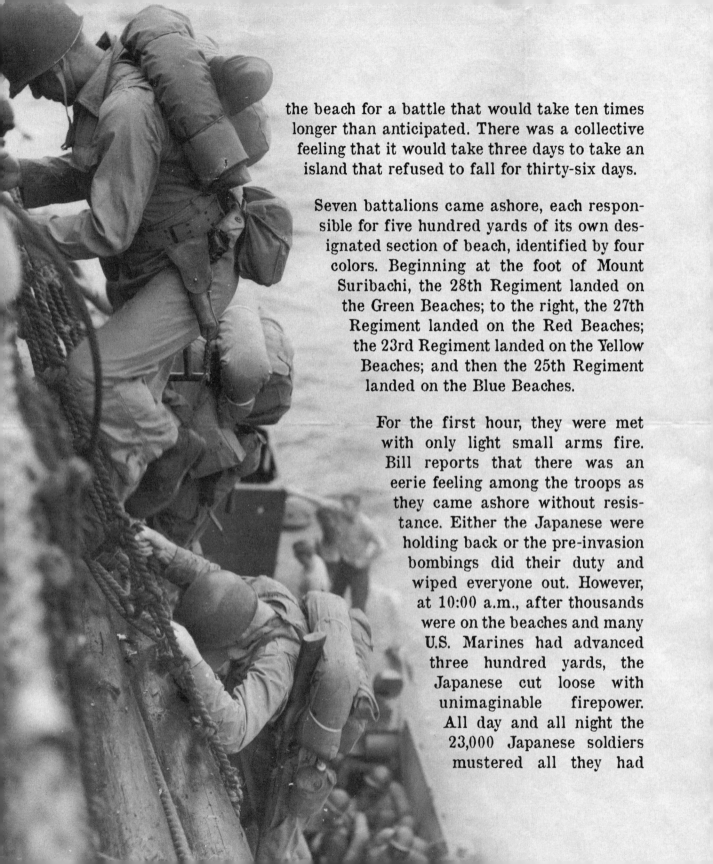

the beach for a battle that would take ten times longer than anticipated. There was a collective feeling that it would take three days to take an island that refused to fall for thirty-six days.

Seven battalions came ashore, each responsible for five hundred yards of its own designated section of beach, identified by four colors. Beginning at the foot of Mount Suribachi, the 28th Regiment landed on the Green Beaches; to the right, the 27th Regiment landed on the Red Beaches; the 23rd Regiment landed on the Yellow Beaches; and then the 25th Regiment landed on the Blue Beaches.

For the first hour, they were met with only light small arms fire. Bill reports that there was an eerie feeling among the troops as they came ashore without resistance. Either the Japanese were holding back or the pre-invasion bombings did their duty and wiped everyone out. However, at 10:00 a.m., after thousands were on the beaches and many U.S. Marines had advanced three hundred yards, the Japanese cut loose with unimaginable firepower. All day and all night the 23,000 Japanese soldiers mustered all they had and rained down artillery fire upon the Marines, trying to push them back into the sea. We had 5,372 casualties in the first two days of battle—1,722 of them during the daylight hours of D+2 alone—three men dying almost every minute.[1]

For over a month, Bill fought on very little rest, and miraculously lived through the entire battle. His outfit won international notoriety when they raised the flag on Mount Suribachi and gave us one of the most famous photos in the history of photography. He tells about the walk back to the ships after the last day of the battle:

> Finally, on March 26 we secured the island and they gave us orders to pick up our gear. We were going to be evacuated and taken back to our base camp. We struggled down the road, a rag-tag bunch, and a miserable-looking outfit.
>
> No other outfit had ever seen combat for 37 days of intense direct conflict quite like Iwo Jima. In other long battles, the conflict would go on for a few days and then back off, but not on Iwo Jima. No one had shaved for five weeks. Of course, I was crusted with sweat and rain and volcanic ash dried on. We were a crummy-looking outfit. Our eyes were sunken from lack of sleep; blurred from the horrors we had seen.
>
> As we marched down the beach, we detoured around to go by the Fifth Marine Division's cemetery. At first we were stumbling along, but as we got closer to that cemetery I noticed something happening. The men started to march more erectly. They formed themselves up in order, and instead of stumbling on, they were marching. Those who were limping, no longer limped. When we got to the cemetery, everyone was marching ramrod straight. Something had happened to them. There was a sense of awe and reverence. As I left I saw an epitaph which was written on an ammunitions carton. It is engraved on my mind. It read:

'WHEN YOU GO HOME, TELL THEM FOR US AND SAY, FOR YOUR TOMORROW, WE GAVE OUR TODAY.'

Bill continues, "To give you the magnitude of it, it took twenty-two ships to bring our division to Iwo Jima, it only took eight to take us home."

It was an island of sacrifice.

Securing Iwo Jima allowed our country to wage a successful bombardment of Japan which finally led to her downfall.

But there was more. These costly sacrifices saved the lives of over 24,000 Army Air Corps airmen who were returning from battle with damaged airplanes, who would have plunged into the ocean if Iwo Jima was not secured by the United States Marines.

The deeds of valor on Iwo Jima are illustrations of a situation where the sacrifice of one group secured a future for another. This is the nature of war, and it is the nature of biblical manhood. The statement, "All gave some, but some gave all," is one of those phrases that communicates the idea that war requires various levels of sacrifice. Some soldiers sacrifice what are regarded as small things, while others make what we call the ultimate sacrifice—death. This is true with wartime, but it is especially true with God's design for manhood. Wartime means that money and time and relationships and even emotions be spent differently. You use less gasoline and food because the resources are needed for the battle. In World War II, the entire U.S. population participated in a massive rationing program that allocated only small amounts of what today we would call "necessities."

The privations were legendary. There were scrap metal drives to build more weapons and old tire drives to provide more rubber. Gasoline, sugar, bread, and meat were rationed according to the size of one's family. Common everyday pleasures were given up to support a wartime economy, to secure a future.

Our troops on Iwo Jima were sacrificing for their families, sweethearts, businesses, and way of life back home. Those same kinds of sacrifices need to be made today. Every generation has its unique defining battles where one group must sacrifice for another. I believe that one of the defining battles of the twenty-first century is the battle for the biblical role of manhood. One aspect of this battle is to wrestle with men to convince them to rise up and prepare their sons for battle.

Iwo Jima brings to mind the sacrifices men must make to win the battle for the family. Today, the family, the foundation of human society, is being dashed on the rocks and undermined by nearly every celebrity, institution, and philosophy. Sons and daughters are being lost through the neglect of their fathers. In times like these, a father must give his today for the tomorrow of his children. Men must rise up with a holy vision and set aside their preferences, entertainments, and selfish patterns.

A Father Must

1. PROVIDE SPECIFIC BIBLICAL INSTRUCTION ON THE MATTER.

Fathers can help their sons understand the nature of biblical manhood and self-sacrifice by instructing them in what the Bible says about manhood. The self-esteem movement has created a generation of young people who treat self-satisfaction as prudent and good. Selfishness has been idolized and shamelessly promoted. Quite naturally, the result is a style-driven, debt-laden people which have unscrupulously murdered millions of its own children. A father's only hope is to read the Bible to his son and explain the whole counsel of God on biblical manhood.

2. SPEND TIME DIFFERENTLY.

Fathers should consider redirecting their energies and using their time differently, dying to themselves in order for the next generation to prosper spiritually.

3. FIGHT FOR THE PRESERVATION OF HIS FAMILY.

The destroyers of biblical manhood are lurking everywhere—including in the church. The fight against them must include the issue of a detailed challenge. Challenge your son to a lifestyle which will make him boldly and effectively recover biblical manhood. Lost in our culture are fathers who put aside their pet agendas and walk beside their children and communicate the doctrines of sin, judgment, righteousness, and the love of God when they sit in their house, when they walk by the way, when they lie down, and when they rise up (Deuteronomy 6:6-8). Who will lead the way? It must be our sons who have been instructed in particular, countercultural, biblical patterns.

4. KEEP THE FAMILY TOGETHER.

Stop outsourcing your son. Instead of personally walking beside our sons, the current practice of almost every family is to outsource them to the video game, the DVD, the internet, the music stream, the coach, the college. Fathers today cast their children out in the great broad road, and there, absent of personal fatherly discipleship, wisdom, love, and correction, they fall. Consider that there are millions of children in our land who have been outsourced, simply because everyone else is doing it. In our land there are millions of outsourced boys in a freefall, whose only hope is the gospel, with no one to pull them "out of the fire, hating even the garment defiled by the flesh" (Jude 23).

Make sure he understands the heart—the main point—of biblical manhood illustrated in the statement "...as Christ loved the church and gave Himself for her" (Ephesians 5:25). Don't let him ever forget the lines scrawled on that ammunitions carton at the Fifth Division cemetery. It should be a reminder that sacrifice is necessary to secure a hope for our children. On Iwo Jima, our troops gave up everything so that freedom would be preserved. My prayer is that there would be an uprising of fathers like the warriors on Iwo Jima, who will give their todays, for the tomorrows of the next generation.

Train your sons to train their own sons, who will train their sons, who will train their sons, for a thousand generations.

"Son, Sacrifice for the Next Generation"

EVERY SON NEEDS TO HEAR
HIS FATHER SAY:
"Son, Make Long and Loyal Friendships"

Do not forsake your own friend or your father's friend.

- Proverbs 27:10

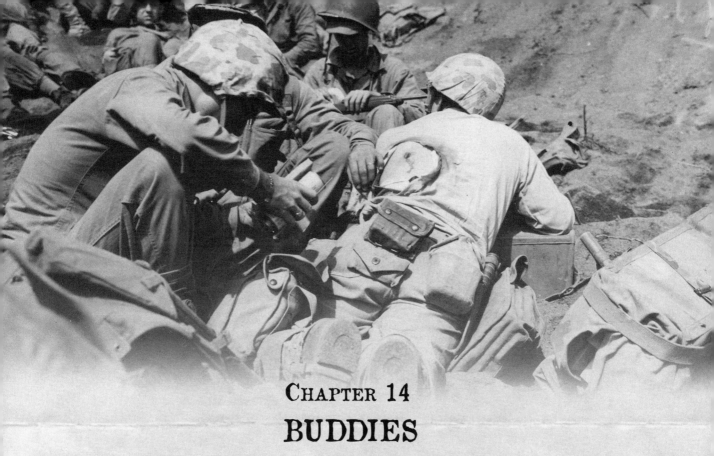

CHAPTER 14

BUDDIES

A father must teach his son the biblical roadmap of friendship, for it is with friends that they will share the journey.

The Bible makes a big deal of friendship. Abraham was the "friend of God," and Christ was the "friend of sinners." Christ defined the terms of friendship more clearly than anyone ever did when He said, "Greater love has no one than this than to lay down one's life for his friends" (John 15:13). Preparing sons for friendship means communicating biblical teaching on the subject and demonstrating it in everyday life. Some of these principles of friendship were illustrated in interesting ways during the battle for Iwo Jima.

It was sixty years after the end of the war when I finally met my father's best friend on Iwo. Arthur Burry. After spending a few hours with him in my father's house, it was easy to see why they were friends. They keyed off of one another perfectly, and humor rolled out its welcome mat. The peals of laughter among friends are always good medicine. And boy did we laugh! For many years, I heard about this mythical man, Burry, and the adventures they had together. There is an amazing chemistry between men when they have endured hardship together in battle. Something forges their souls together, causing remembrances until the day they die. I believe this is a gift from heaven, for it is God who gives us friends; God who provides laughter and camaraderie.

Arthur, my Dad and I had three days together. We spent a lot of time talking about Iwo Jima and airplanes...and friendship.

Since boyhood, my father told me of the harrowing experiences Burry had with his airplanes. We would laugh together as he recounted the different planes he tore up. So when we met, I just had to ask Burry how many planes he wrecked. He said, "I think maybe one."

I turned to my dad, "I thought you said that Burry tore up lots of planes."

Burry responded, "Well, now that I think about it, there was that one, but that was immaterial." One plane, huh?

The next day I asked, "Burry, we want to know about the planes you crashed and the lessons you learned."

He said, "Apparently, after the first one, I didn't learn much."

"So how many did you crash?" I pressed.

He replied, "I really don't know. Well, one plane was damaged when I was on a low-flying training mission in a P51. I followed my flight leader into power lines, hitting the propeller and putting a crease on the leading edge of both wings. But I don't count that one because I was following my flight leader."

Now we were up to two planes.

On the third day, after wearing him down for more stories, he told me that he "also lost a plane during gunnery training in Long Island. That one really doesn't count either because we were in training. I don't remember much about that one. The engine quit and I had to crash land ("pancake in") in a potato field without wheels down. The farmer called the base and they came and picked me up." Burry may not remember much, but my dad recalls that when they came to get him, they found him sitting on the wing smoking a cigar. The farmer sent the USAAF a bill for damages to the crops, because heavy trucks had to come in and drive all over his potato field trying to get the airframe off the farm.

That made three.

"Any more?" I asked.

He confided, "Well, another time, in a P47, my brakes went out and I plowed into another airplane at Bellows Field, so I wouldn't really count that one, would you?"

I was ruthless, "I think I count that as five wrecked planes."

"Rats," he said.

It was time to own up.

"Then there was the time I dumped a plane in the ocean and floated in the Pacific for six days," he continued. "I would not count that one either because the engine just quit running." Then he added, "When you take off, anything can happen."

That makes six planes!

I laughed so much hearing Burry's commentary, and the growing list of plane wrecks, that I nearly lost count. He had flown and crashed several of the most powerful, expensive, and collectible planes in history and, in his words, it was "immaterial," "all in a days work."

One day he was flying in a P47 off of Bellows Field in Hawaii just before they went to Iwo Jima when the engine quit again! He found a spot to land on the top of a mountain, and on the way in, got tangled up in some telephone wires which severed some telephone poles. His plane screeched to a halt—just a few feet away from the edge of a giant cliff. If that weren't enough, he had just knocked out Admiral Nimitz's radio communications with North America.

SEVEN wrecked planes.

I thought of the humor and the understatement that somehow must have been the cartilage of his relationship with my easy-going father. I can see why they were friends. They both love to laugh and they are a delight to those around them.

As I think about my father on Iwo Jima, I know for certain that even through the death and carnage and fire, there was a gift from God that oiled the situations and friendships there. Affinity and laughter between a man and his friends are grace given from God in the midst of a sometimes harsh and disappointing world. God is the originator of these things.

THE POWER OF FRIENDSHIP

It is strange how friends affect one another. They take you in directions that you can never anticipate and then profoundly affect your life. It is vitally important to choose them carefully. For example, it was the various powers of friendship that led to the writing of this book.

Many years ago I started holding Memorial Day celebrations on our farm to honor those who died in service to our country. At the first event, my friend Jim Dyer, a veteran of Vietnam, came to share his story from the platform. Sometime after that first celebration, he dropped by my office, put a cassette tape on my desk, and said, "You have to listen to this!" I threw it in my briefcase and went off with my wife to spend the weekend at the beach. On the way, we listened to the tape. I was floored by the story of a local Marine named Bill Henderson who, for the first time in his life, publicly told the story of his experience on Iwo Jima. He did it reluctantly at the urging of his pastor and a few of his friends, such as Bill Delahoyde. I was so captivated by his story, that I spent the entire weekend transcribing the tape into a written manuscript.

After listening to the audio recording that Jim gave me, I felt that I had to meet the man who gave that speech. Jim gave me Bill's phone number and we arranged a meeting. We had lunch together and immediately struck up a friendship. One day later on, I met him at his office and he showed me several original documents and maps that he had with him on Iwo. That was the day I asked him if he knew any other local men who had been on Iwo Jima. He said, "You probably don't know Buck Bunn, but he was a B-29 pilot there."

That led to my discovery of the connection between Buck Bunn's wartime experiences and the downing of my father's plane.

I then introduced my friends Bill Henderson and Buck Bunn to my good friend, Doug Phillips, who became interested in their stories—so interested, in fact, that I decided to fly Bill and his wife and my father and mother to Fredericksburg Texas to put them in front of a camera so that Doug could interview them. This ultimately led to our trip to the island of Iwo Jima, which was primarily a result of the visionary thinking of Doug Phillips. When you match ordinary men who have stories to tell with men with a gigantic vision, like Doug, watch out!—something remarkable is about to happen.

While we were doing the interviews in Fredericksburg, Doug asked the men if they would be willing to return to Iwo. This was an interesting question because of the complex logistical difficulties, the costs, and the time involved. One barrier is that Iwo Jima is under the control of the Japanese government, and they permit American citizens to tour the island only one day per year—and only during daylight hours.

Both Bill Henderson and my father were adamant; they were NOT going back to Iwo. I will never forget Bill Henderson saying, "No, thank you, I have already visited Iwo Jima." A year later I asked him again if he would

go and he said in no uncertain terms, "Been there, done that!" Then, a few months later, for some strange reason both Bill and my father agreed to make the journey for the 60th anniversary of the battle. Doug and I breathed a big sigh of relief—mixed with a gasp of fear—because we were hardly sure how we could pull it off. It would be an epic journey that would consume significant resources and time.

Remember—choose your friends wisely, for you will key off of one another and they will take you in directions you might not have anticipated or even wanted. You also need to be careful about doing the same to them.

This is why we should have friends who have great and godly thoughts. May we be positively impressed by those thoughts! On the other hand, if we choose small-minded or worldly friends, we might be directed in ways we shouldn't go.

All these friendships began with a simple Memorial Day celebration. One friendship multiplied to many and ended up bringing together dozens of other men who would be forever changed by their mutual affections and interests. This would lead to the preservation of a godly heritage through the recounting of historical events from a providential historical perspective.

A Father Must

1. TEACH HIS SON THAT FRIENDSHIP IS A GIFT OF GOD.

The blessing of friendship is expressed in Proverbs 27:9, "Ointment and perfume delight the heart, and the sweetness of a man's friend gives delight by hearty counsel." God provides many gifts in life and friendship is one that eases many of the bumps and bruises that come upon us. Sometimes friendship has a sharpening effect, as Proverbs 27:17 reveals, "As iron sharpens iron, So a man sharpens the countenance of his friend." Not only do friendships sharpen, they sometimes inflict wounds that turn out to be emblems of faithfulness, as Proverbs 27:6 describes, "Faithful are the wounds of a friend, But the kisses of an enemy are deceitful." Unfortunately, some men choose to be loners and deprive themselves of these gifts. Often, they go through their whole life and never break the habit of avoiding friendships. They end up living lives without cultivating something that God has provided for their comfort, their counsel, and for the expansion of His kingdom. A father must be aware of this danger and help his children to avoid it.

2. HELP HIS SON UNDERSTAND THAT FRIENDSHIPS ARE VALUABLE, NOT BECAUSE THEY ARE ALWAYS SMOOTH, BUT BECAUSE THEY SERVE TO TEST LOVE AND LOYALTY.

Friendship is tested when things happen that tempt us to cultivate feelings of dishonor and lack of love toward a friend. When we discover personality differences or lapses in the spiritual lives of our friends, we are tested. What will we do? How will we handle the information we have about our friend? The temptation is to despise the friend. Instead of looking at their quirks as terms of endearment and the lapses in their lives as opportunities to pour on more love and more heartfelt prayer, we often allow those things to separate us. This is one reason Proverbs 27:10 counsels, "Do not forsake your own friend or your father's friend." When friendship is tested, we must remember the counsel of Paul, "Love does not keep an account of wrongs suffered" (I Corinthians 13:1-3), and the original "Peter principle," "Love covers a multitude of sins" (I Peter 4:8).

3. HELP HIS SON REALIZE THAT TO HAVE FRIENDS, HE MUST BE FRIENDLY (PROVERBS 18:24).

This was a favorite saying of my grandfather and he quoted it when he observed someone who did not reach out in friendship. This confirms my observation that the men I know who have friends are initiators of friendship. The friendless are always waiting around for someone to befriend them. When it doesn't happen, they keep walking down the loaner track. However, God's way is better; He calls us to be friendly and to make friendships happen.

4. SHOW HIS SON THE IMPORTANCE OF CHOOSING FRIENDS CAREFULLY.

I believe that in some senses Christian men ought to be the friends of all men, but for our closest friends, Scripture makes it clear that there should be some discrimination, and prioritization. Proverbs 22:24 says, "Make no friendship with an angry man, And with a furious man do not go." Friends have an enormous influence on us, which is why Paul said to the Corinthian church, "Do not be deceived: 'Evil company corrupts good habits'" (1 Corinthians 15:33).

For these reasons, I will teach my son to look for three things in his closest friends, which I hope will mark the characteristics of his own friendliness. First, look for the fruits of the Spirit. Do they demonstrate a Spirit-directed life? Second, how do they impact others? Do they encourage love and good deeds in us? Third, do they sincerely promote a holy lifestyle and stimulate in us a desire for holiness instead of worldliness? The flip side is also true: not only should our sons look for these qualities in others, but they ought to strive to provide these same things for their friends as well.

5. SHOW HIS SON HOW TO MAINTAIN LONG AND LOYAL FRIENDSHIPS.

Friends are sometimes tempted to betrayal, which has devastating results both socially and in our relationship with God. Psalm 15:3 speaks of those who will be allowed into the presence of the Lord, "He who does not backbite with his tongue, nor does evil to his neighbor, nor does he take up a reproach against his friend." Taking up a reproach against a friend has serious consequences. Paul tells Timothy that you will sometimes find "traitors" and "slanderers" in the church. They are wolves in sheep's clothing, according to 2 Timothy 3:3-5. David lamented this problem when he said, "Even my own familiar friend in whom I trusted, who ate my bread, has lifted up his heel against me" (Psalm 41:9). We are actually commanded to maintain long friendships as is indicated in Proverbs 27:10, "Do not forsake your own friend or your father's friend."

6. WARN HIS SON ABOUT BECOMING LIKE JOB'S FRIENDS.

Job's friends presumed to know why things were happening to him. Friends often judge one another, because they think they know their friends' hearts. They wrongfully believe they know why difficulty has befallen him. They use it to criticize. My experience is when friends take this route, after a while, they almost always look back upon it as a mistake. Job's friends were unmerciful toward him. They wrongfully judged him. They did not know that God was doing something to test Job and to demonstrate His own glory. Job's friends belittled him at the lowest point in his life. When he desperately needed their encouragement, they kicked him. That was their

legacy in friendship. Now as you read this story, four thousand years after the events, Job is the hero and his friends are the goats. The lesson from Job is this: When your friend is down, don't presume he has sinned and don't presume you know the secrets of what is happening—pray the prayer of David, "Keep back your servant also from presumptuous sins, let them not have dominion over me...Let the words of my mouth and the mediations of my heart be acceptable in Thy sight..." (Psalm 19:13,14).

7. HELP HIS SON BECOME A LOW-MAINTENANCE FRIEND.

High-maintenance friends are always demanding of time and attention and are offended if they don't get their share. Their desire for attention sometimes clouds their judgment and they make themselves a burden instead of an inspiration. Proverbs 27:14 speaks of one characteristic of a high-maintenance friend who demands attention in inappropriate ways, "He who blesses his friend with a loud voice, rising early in the morning, it will be counted a curse to him." Low-maintenance friends are the kind of friends who can pick up where they left off and do not smother. Teach your son to be the kind of friend who is happy that his friends have other friends. Teach him to be content regardless of whether or not he was included in something that his friend was. Teach him to be selfless. Self-love is usually the culprit in a high-maintenance friendship.

8. WARN HIS SON TO AVOID SURETY FOR A FRIEND.

Proverbs 17:18 makes it clear that making yourself responsible for a friend's debts is a sign of foolishness in friendship, for "A man devoid of understanding shakes hands in a pledge, And becomes surety for his friend." Friends should avoid getting entangled financially, especially by becoming liable for one another's obligations. Further, I generally counsel men that partnerships are a bad idea. They seldom turn out well and they always open friends to pressures that may ultimately destroy the friendship.

9. EXPLAIN TO HIS SON THAT THE MOST IMPORTANT PERSONALITY TO TEACH US ABOUT FRIENDSHIP IS THE LORD JESUS CHRIST.

John reports that Jesus said to His disciples, "No longer do I call you servants, for a servant does not know what his master is doing; but I have called you friends, for all things that I heard from My Father I have made known to you" (John 15:15). The Lord Jesus demonstrates the best qualities of friendship a man can ever have, for "There is a friend who sticks closer than a brother" (Proverbs 18:24). The implication is that Christ sticks closer to us than even a brother. This teaches us that friends can even be closer than relatives, which contradicts the statement, "Blood is thicker than water."

10. UNDERSTAND THAT CHRIST FULFILLS ALL THE REQUIREMENTS OF EXEMPLARY FRIENDSHIP.

Jesus Christ is our supreme example of friendship for He is both holy and happy. The writer of Hebrews describes him as having "loved righteousness and hated lawlessness; therefore God, Your God, has anointed You with the oil of gladness more than Your companions" (Hebrews 1:9). Without trivializing His character or His mighty Name or His perfect holiness, I think we can say with confidence that the Lord Jesus Christ was the best and happiest of friends anyone ever had. In this sense, it is appropriate for us to pray that the Lord will make us happy friends.

Scripture gives us many words and relationships that are meant to help us to define the terms of friendship and give us examples to follow. Paul, writing to Philemon, captures the kinds of friendships that God can create in His church, "Paul...to Philemon our beloved friend and fellow laborer" (Philemon 1:1). May God give us beloved friends and fellow laborers, and may we also be these kinds of friends.

This is one of the most powerful legacies my father has given to our family.

There is nothing like a happy father...and a faithful friend!

A cheerful heart is good medicine. (Proverbs 17:22)

"Son, Make Long and Loyal Friendships"

EVERY SON NEEDS TO HEAR

HIS FATHER SAY:

"Son, Flee Immorality"

Flee also youthful lusts; but pursue righteousness, faith, love, peace with those who call on the Lord out of a pure heart.

- I Timothy 2:22

CHAPTER 15

BOXES FROM HOME

Helping your son deal with temptation is one of the most important things a father ever does, for in this world temptation is always just around the corner. The boys on Iwo Jima faced the temptations that every boy faces. This was revealed in a very powerful moment when Bill Henderson was telling about his experience in the Pacific war. He spoke of the temptations that they all faced, and the things that made some able to flee, and others ready to fall. When you are away from home and fall into boredom and then are subjected to pressure, the weaknesses of the flesh, and the weaknesses of men around you, sexual sin can overtake you—unless you have been strengthened against it. Wartime always delivers unusual temptations which is why Moses said, "When the army goes out against your enemies, then keep yourself from every wicked thing" (Deuteronomy 23:9).

Bill Henderson remembers getting letters and goodies from his mother which she packaged up in beautifully assembled wooden boxes. His father had carefully made each box especially for him. He tells of how his father and mother made sure everything about the boxes breathed of their love for him. It was their way of saying, "I'm proud of you and I love you and I'm praying for you." Bill speaks of the impact of these boxes and the connections they made in his own words,

What I saw in my father's relationship with my mother helped me not do some things others were doing. I'd go out with the guys, and frankly we'd go to some places we shouldn't have gone. We'd go to what we called "comfort houses," they were "whore houses" to tell it like it is. I would never go in and be serviced. I would wait for the men who went in. I'd talk to some of the girls, but I'd never participate. One Singapore madam asked me not to come back anymore, because I'd talk to the girls, and two of her girls had quit. I would say, "Honey, why are you doing this?" I said this because I really was compassionate toward them. I've always had a very high opinion of women. The very idea, that they would do this is very distasteful to me. To think that a women would give of herself like that, giving one of her most precious gifts, just time and time again, just was so distasteful to me, that I talked to the girls about it. And so she finally asked me not to come back any more because two of her girls had quit and gone home because of it. This happened because of my mother's and father's relationship; I knew if my father thought that I did something like that, it would just break his heart."

It was the love of a father and mother that helped Bill keep his wits about him when both the devil and his hormones were attacking him. While Bill was almost ten thousand miles away, his father and mother were counseling him with loving acts of kindness and it was effective. Their simple wooden boxes were used by the Holy Spirit to help their son to "Abstain from fleshly lusts which wage war against the soul" (I Peter 2:9-12).

Bill's experience in the Pacific serves as a reminder that fathers must step up and give clear instructions to help their sons deal with this threat, for it is a threat that will chase them all over the world.

The book of Proverbs makes it clear that because she (lust) is convenient (Proverbs 5) and aggressive (Genesis 39), the only reasonable action for a father is to take time to assist his son in this most dangerous territory.

A Father Must

1. COMMUNICATE THE PRINCIPLE OF MORTIFYING LUST.

Here is the principle: Because lust grows when it is fed, starve it. Feeding sexual sin causes lust to grow to where it finally overtakes us. Richard Baxter gives this directive: "Keep as far as you can from those temptations which feed and strengthen the sins which you would overcome...Lay siege to your sins, and starve them out, by keeping away the food and fuel which is their maintenance and life."[1]

Lust can be weakened, but this only happens when there is enough hatred of sin to starve it out.

2. CLARIFY THE RESULTS OF FAILURE.

Because sin is death and immorality is sin, so immorality is death. Solomon understood this death grip with perfect clarity in Proverbs 7:

With her enticing speech she caused him to yield, with her flattering lips she seduced him. Immediately he went after her, as an ox goes to the slaughter, or as a fool to the correction of the stocks, till an arrow struck his liver. As a bird hastens to the snare, he did not know it would cost his life. Now therefore, listen to me, my children; pay attention to the words of my mouth: do not let your heart turn aside to her ways, do not stray into her paths; for she has cast down many wounded, and all who were slain by her were strong men. Her house is the way to hell, descending to the chambers of death. (Proverbs 7:21-27)

Immorality spells death to a host of relationships and opportunities. There so much at stake when purity is compromised.

John Owen explains the consequences of sin in this way, "How few are there that walk in any beauty or glory! How barren, how useless they are, for the most part!...Many men harbor spirit-devouring lusts in their bosoms, that lie as worms at the root of their obedience, and corrode and weaken it day by day...God blasts such men's undertakings."[2] Remember Lot and how his compromises cost him everything, and David whose succumbing plunged him into the depths of despair and robbed him of future fruitfulness. And don't forget the contrast we see in Joseph whose integrity saved him and promoted him far beyond imagination.

2 Peter 2:10-22 exposes many of the dangers of lust,

... those who walk according to the flesh in the lust of uncleanness and despise authority. They are presumptuous, self-willed. They are not afraid to speak evil of dignitaries, whereas angels, who are greater in power and might, do not bring a reviling accusation against them before the Lord. But these, like natural brute beasts made to be caught and destroyed, speak evil of the things they do not understand, and will utterly perish in their own corruption, and will receive the wages of unrighteousness, as those who count it pleasure to carouse in the daytime. They are spots and blemishes, carousing in their own deceptions while they feast with you, having eyes full of adultery and that cannot cease from sin, enticing unstable souls. They have a heart trained in covetous practices, and are accursed children. They have forsaken the right way and gone astray, following the way of Balaam the son of Beor, who loved the wages of unrighteousness; but he was rebuked for his iniquity: a dumb donkey speaking with a man's voice restrained the madness of the prophet. These are wells without water, clouds carried by a tempest, for whom is reserved the blackness of darkness forever. For when they speak great swelling words of emptiness, they allure through the lusts of the flesh, through lewdness, the ones who have actually escaped from those who live in error. While they promise them liberty, they themselves are slaves of corruption; for by whom a person is overcome, by him also he is brought into bondage. For if, after they have escaped the pollutions of the world through the knowledge of the Lord and Savior Jesus Christ, they are again entangled in them and overcome, the latter end is worse for them than the beginning. For it would have been better for them not to have known the way of righteousness, than having known it, to turn from the holy commandment delivered to them. But it has happened to them according to the true proverb: 'A dog returns to his own vomit', and, 'a sow, having washed, to her wallowing in the mire.'"

3. EXPLAIN THE DRAMATIC ACTIONS THAT NEED TO BE TAKEN TO HAVE SUCCESS.

Jesus explained the radical response we ought to have regarding sin in Matthew 18:7-10:

Woe to the world because of offenses! For offenses must come, but woe to that man by whom the offense comes! If your hand or foot causes you to sin, cut it off and cast it from you. It is better for you to enter into life lame or maimed, rather than having two hands or two feet, to be cast into the everlasting fire. And if your eye causes you to sin, pluck it out and cast it from you. It is better for you to enter into life with one eye, rather than having two eyes, to be cast into hell fire. Take heed that you do not despise one of these little ones, for I say to you that in heaven their angels always see the face of My Father who is in heaven."

4. HELP HIS SON TO ESTABLISH HOLY MANAGEMENT OF THE EYES AND EARS THAT WILL WORK ON AUTO-PILOT WHEREVER HE MIGHT BE.

Lust will attack you wherever you are. You must be ready. Readiness to subdue the attack of lust is something that must be cultivated.

One of the problems we have in this area is that we live in an era where nearly everyone opens eyes and ears for things unlawful in the eyes of God. So, if we ever hope to protect our eyes, we will have to realize that we won't be looking at and listening to what everyone else does.

Ephesians 5:3-14 gives us clear principles for governing eyes and ears,

> But fornication and all uncleanness or covetousness, let it not even be named among you, as is fitting for saints; neither filthiness, nor foolish talking, nor coarse

jesting, which are not fitting, but rather giving of thanks. For this you know, that no fornicator, unclean person, nor covetous man, who is an idolater, has any inheritance in the kingdom of Christ and God. Let no one deceive you with empty words, for because of these things the wrath of God comes upon the sons of disobedience. Therefore do not be partakers with them. For you were once darkness, but now you are light in the Lord. Walk as children of light (for the fruit of the Spirit is in all goodness, righteousness, and truth), finding out what is acceptable to the Lord. And have no fellowship with the unfruitful works of darkness, but rather expose them. For it is shameful even to speak of those things which are done by them in secret. But all things that are exposed are made manifest by the light, for whatever makes manifest is light.Therefore He says: 'Awake, you who sleep, Arise from the dead, And Christ will give you light.'"

Psalm 101:3 addresses the eyes and their use in the house,

I will set nothing wicked before my eyes; I hate the work of those who fall away; it shall not cling to me.

Job explains his personal method for managing his eyes,

I have made a covenant with my eyes; why then should I look upon a young woman?... Is it not destruction for the wicked, and disaster for the workers of iniquity? Does He not see my ways, and count all my steps?...If my heart has been enticed by a woman, or if I have lurked at my neighbor's door, then let my wife grind for another, and let others bow down over her. For that would be wickedness; yes, it would be iniquity deserving of judgment. For that would be a fire that consumes to destruction, and would root out all my increase." (Job 31:1,34,9,10)

James issues a command that requires that we lay aside filthiness and receive the implanted Word,

Therefore lay aside all filthiness and overflow of wickedness, and receive with meekness the implanted word, which is able to save your souls." (James 1:21)

What eyes see and ears hear molds the affections. The Puritan William Fenner said that we grow affections, and they in turn take us wherever they

want. Affections matter. They have the ability to control us. Paul spoke of the mighty power of affections:

> We have spoken openly to you, Corinthians; our heart has been opened wide. You are not limited by us, but you are limited by your own affections. Now in like response—I speak as to children—you also should be open to us. Do not be mismatched with unbelievers. For what partnership is there between righteousness and lawlessness? Or what fellowship does light have with darkness? What agreement does Christ have with Belial? Or what does a believer have in common with an unbeliever? And what agreement does God's sanctuary have with idols? For we are the sanctuary of the living God, as God said: I will dwell among them and walk among them, and I will be their God, and they will be My people. Therefore, come out from among them and be separate, says the Lord; do not touch any unclean thing, and I will welcome you. I will be a Father to you, and you will be sons and daughters to Me, says the Lord Almighty. (I Corinthians 6:11-18)

5. BE THE REMINDER OF THE LAW OF LOVE.

One aspect of love is summed up in the statement, "Do unto others as you would have them do unto you" (Matthew 7:12). Every opportunity for fornication or adultery is an opportunity to act in selfish hatred (lack of love) for our neighbor. If a man fornicates or commits adultery, he always violates the law of love because he sins with someone else's daughter or wife. You would not want anyone trifling with your daughter. Remembering the law of love is an opportunity to do unto others as you would have them do unto you. Because all of God's commandments are summed up by love, the Tenth Commandment must also be obeyed:

> You shall not covet your neighbor's house; you shall not covet your neighbor's wife, nor his male servant, nor his female servant, nor his ox, nor his donkey, nor anything that is your neighbor's." (Exodus 20:17)

6. BE CLEAR ABOUT THE SINFULNESS OF VIRTUAL IMMORALITY.

There may be some who think that virtual fornication or adultery is not the same as physical sin. This kind of thinking is based on the mistaken belief that it is actual physical contact that is immoral, but that the internet is a "free" zone because it is "virtual." Does fornication before marriage or cheating during marriage require physical contact? The problem is that modern technology allows men to have virtual internet harems.

Computerized fornication over the internet is just as bad as real, live, old-fashioned infidelity. In simplest terms, it cultivates virtual girlfriends with whom you virtually fornicate, or if you are married, adulterous relationships that are nothing less than actual adulteries of the mind. Jesus explained it this way,

> But I say to you that whoever looks at a woman to lust for her has already committed adultery with her in his heart. (Matthew 5:28)

> And if your eye causes you to sin, pluck it out and cast it from you. It is better for you to enter into life with one eye, rather than having two eyes, to be cast into hell fire. (Matthew 18:9)

7. BE CLEAR THAT SELF-GRATIFICATION IS WRONG.

Whether you are simply thinking about or actually looking on a woman, self-gratification carries the soul in the wrong direction. It always involves feeding your lust. The more you do anything, the more you will want it. Therefore, self-gratification draws you in the direction you don't want to go. This action never drew anyone to more purity or more holiness but always in the other direction. Not only that, but as it pulls you along, it intensifies instead of relieves. I have heard people say that it lets off sexual tension that builds up like a volcano. This is a lie. On the contrary, it builds sexual tension to another level not yet known. It does not decrease unlawful sexual desire, it inflames and feeds it.

I believe that pornography, whether virtual as previously mentioned or a video or magazine or anything else, belongs in the same category because it is the creation of an intimate partner or "looking upon a woman" who has not been allowed by God under the authority of His Word.

8. REMIND HIS SON OF THE BLESSINGS PROMISED FOR OBEDIENCE.

Deuteronomy 28:1-6 documents a long list of blessings that come from obedience:

> Now it shall come to pass, if you diligently obey the voice of the Lord your God, to observe carefully all His commandments which I command you today, that the Lord your God will set you high above all nations of the earth. And all these blessings shall come upon you and overtake you, because you obey the voice of the Lord your God: Blessed shall you be in the city, and blessed shall you be in the country. Blessed shall be the fruit of your body, the produce of your ground and the increase of your herds, the increase of your cattle and the offspring of your flocks. Blessed shall be your basket and your kneading bowl. Blessed shall you be when you come in, and blessed shall you be when you go out."

9. BE LIKE CHRIST IN PURITY.

> Therefore let us cast off the works of darkness, and let us put on the armor of light. Let us walk properly, as in the day, not in revelry and drunkenness, not in lewdness and lust, not in strife and envy. But put on the Lord Jesus Christ, and make no provision for the flesh, to fulfill its lusts." (Romans 13:12-14)

THE SILVER BULLET.

We have already said that men must take various kinds of actions (such as making a covenant with their eyes) to keep them from sexual temptation. But there is one thing that is of supreme importance and exercises the most power—the work of the Holy Spirit. Paul said in Romans 8:13, "If by the Spirit you mortify the deeds of the flesh, you will live." First notice that there is a condition signified by the word "if." You may or you may not, but "if" you do, you will live. Then he gives the secret of it all—the silver bullet, "by the Spirit." There is no hope without the Holy Spirit at work in our hearts. Submitting to and being filled with the Holy Spirit is the silver bullet against temptation. This is one reason that the grieving of the Holy

Spirit is so bad for us.

A friend of mine sent me a vow that he uses to encourage his children to use so they might see the importance of sexual purity before marriage:

> Believing that God's Word commands me to do so and knowing that God works all things out for my good, I, _____, vow before God, my parents, my family, and my elders to live a life of sexual purity in my thoughts, my will, and my actions. Realizing that God's Word teaches that my body is to be used for my future husband/wife's pleasure and not my own, I will reserve my body and my heart for the future mate God has prepared for me. I will refrain from any form of sexual activity before I am married.
>
> I ask God to bring misery and pain to my life if I do not strive with all my heart to keep this vow. I furthermore vow to make myself accountable to my parents in this area my affirming to them monthly that I am upholding my vow. I vow to be honest in my affirmations and ask God to bring pain and misery to me if I lie about my affirmation.

I don't think that written vows are required, but at least you can see that that the man who used the above vow desired to clarify his desire for sexual purity.

Bill Henderson reported that it was his father's love for his mother that helped him keep out of the brothels in the Pacific. He saw the blessings of purity in his home. He observed the chaste behavior of his mother and the love of his father for her. It was faith in action—theology visualized. Perhaps this is one reason that marriage is intended by God to explain Christ's love for the church. "Husbands, love your wives as also Christ loved the church and gave Himself up for her" (Ephesians 5:25).

A father's Christ-likeness in marriage is perhaps the most helpful thing he can do for his son. As he loves his wife, his son can see in real life how wonderful Jesus Christ is. As a son sees the blessings of Christ, the love of Christ, and the proper expression of the authority of Christ, he is fortified against evil assaults. Jesus Christ as Lord is the most important motivation for sexual purity.

"Son, Flee Immorality"

EVERY SON NEEDS TO HEAR
HIS FATHER SAY:
"Son, Never Neglect the Local Church"

I write so that you may know how you ought to conduct yourself in the house of God, which is the church of the living God, the pillar and ground of the truth.

- 1 Timothy 3:15

To Him be glory in the church by Christ Jesus to all generations, forever and ever. Amen.

- Ephesians 3:21

CHAPTER 16
THE CHURCH TRIUMPHANT

When people handle precious things with disregard or speak of important things with a casual air, it shows that something is wrong. You wouldn't handle a Stradivarius violin like you would a chainsaw, and you wouldn't handle a newborn baby like you would a football. Different treatments are required, based on the nature and valuation of the object. If a boy would be tempted to take the church lightly, and make her a sideline in his life, he should remember that Christ purchased the church "with his own blood." He calls her His "Bride" (Acts 20:17, Ephesians 5:22-33). The highest price was paid. The church is precious to God. The amazing analogy of a marriage is given, showing us that the church is important to Him. This high valuation (with blood) and tender designation (Bride) ought to make the church a high priority for all boys.

I once asked a Marine who fought on Iwo Jima if he had any recollections of men rising up as true spiritual leaders. His answer was simply, "No."

Most books on the battle have very little to say about this aspect of what occurred.

Even so, Iwo Jima may have been the launching pad for more prayers per square mile than anywhere else in the world in February and March 1945. The 100,000 troops engaged in the battle were facing such horrific circumstances that they had no choice but to cry out to God in prayer. As Paul reminds us in Romans 1, all men know God "...because what may be known of God is manifest in them, for God has shown it to them. For since the creation of the world His invisible attributes are clearly seen, being understood by the things that are made, even His eternal power and Godhead, so that they are without excuse." This is not to say that these prayers were uttered by genuine believers, for many of those men were faithless, yet they prayed in desperation. Where there is violence and insecurity and threats to life, there is almost always a certain brand of sensitivity to eternal things. However, even though it must have been a place of prayer, there seemed to be a marked godlessness about it.

As is true of most war books or documentaries, it is hard to find anything that specifically documents the presence of the church or how the gospel made its appearance through the lives of true believers. The same is true of the battle for Iwo Jima.

But, there is always more than meets the eye. For example, if you go to the National Archives to look at original pictures of the battle, there is a special section called, "Religion." There you will find hundreds of pictures that document at least the outward appearances of religious life on Iwo Jima, of men clinging to expressions of spiritual things. We have already discussed the outworking of their religion in the lives of Bill Brown and Bill Henderson on Iwo Jima, but there are other stories, too.

A Marine from the Fourth Division, by the name of Cornelius Vanderbreggen, Jr., wrote dozens of letters documenting his personal work as an evangelist and disciple-maker as he did his duty in the hospitals of the Pacific war. He was a prayer warrior and evangelist. When Iwo Jima's wounded were brought to Guam, he ministered to them. He prayed, led them in the singing of hymns, and brought them together for Bible study and unashamedly challenged them to repent and believe in the gospel of Christ. He heard many testimonies of the grace of God. He writes,

> "And we rejoice that others have come to call Him wonderful too because of all that God has wrought these past few weeks, as a consequence of Iwo Jima."[1]

Vanderbreggen saw firsthand how the terrors of Iwo Jima were used by the Lord to bring salvation to many of the men who served there. He recalls it this way,

> To the world and to many brave fighting men, Iwo Jima will always be remembered with a sense of horror as the barren volcanic isle where upwards of 20,000 courageous Marines were killed or wounded. "Hell's Acre" is the name that the world has given to it. Yet there is a sequel which should be told of how some of Iwo's casualties, burned, and shell-shocked, and wracked with pain though they were, came to know the living God as a consequence of their experiences; for God by grace used Iwo's terror to help bring them to His Son, Christ Jesus, the Savior of the world. Thus for them "Hell's Acre" has become the very threshold of life eternal."[2]

Not only did the experience on Iwo Jima become a theater for "life eternal," it also exposed the strength of faith:

> Virtually all of the wounded from Iwo Jima told of the unspeakable terror and how frightened they had been...One lad in his teens spoke of the peace they had experienced in battle, the peace that is given in every circumstance to those who are trusting the living God. Had He not said, "Thou shalt not be afraid for the terror by night, nor for the arrow that flieth by day?" These Christian boys agreed that God had kept His word.[3]

He writes further of God's work through His people in the Pacific:

> One boy reported, 'When I was in my foxhole at Iwo Jima,' Tex declared, 'I prayed to God plenty, but it wasn't until two days ago that I found what I have always been looking for. I know now what it means to be a Christian, and I thank God tonight that Christ died for my sins on Calvary...now I belong to the Lord and I know that He will never leave me.'[4]

Sons should be well-prepared for a long, fruitful life among God's people, wherever they might be. This preparation begins with their understanding of the importance of the church in the world and their responsibilities as part of it. The church is explained in some of the most amazing images—the Bride of Christ, the family of God, a building, a body.

A Father Must

1. EXPRESS GOD'S ROLE IN HIS CHURCH.

Every son ought to be aware that the living God is always at work in every inch of the planet to bring people to Himself, and He uses members of His church to do so. No matter how barren the spiritual landscape looks on the surface, God's people are there. There is no place or situation that is out of His reach, no matter how bad circumstances might be. Iwo may have been called "Hell's Acre," but it was under the watchful care of heaven. There were many who were brought into the peace of Jesus Christ through the repentance of their hearts and forgiveness of their sins on the battlefield of Iwo Jima. Peace "like a river" was brought to many in the confusions and desolations of this war.

Even though the popular books and movies do not cover this aspect of the battle, the work of Jesus Christ in the hearts of men were the most important and the most powerful things that were happening there. The church was alive on Iwo Jima even though there were many harsh forces seemingly obscuring it.

2. EXPLAIN HOW THE CHURCH BODY FUNCTIONS.

A father should make his son aware that prayers from the church will be poured out for him if he invests in her people. In America, prayers were constantly being raised on behalf of our boys in Iwo. There were fervent and faithful prayers offered up by the true church of Jesus Christ. They brought their prayers before the throne of God, and He heard the voice of their cries. Even though Iwo Jima was a terrible experience, God heard those prayers and answered them according to His grace and power and everlasting kindness. Many were redeemed by His blood and received a

righteousness which was not their own.

It is interesting that in such a godless place, men were still encouraged to pray before great battles. Before each mission, my father would go to the chaplain's tent to pray.

From all appearances and from many of the testimonies I have heard, the representatives of the true church of Jesus Christ on Iwo Jima seemed to be subdued. But the truth is, there were prayers offered and angels deployed and the church was there on the beaches of Iwo Jima.

In some ways, Iwo was a mirror of normal life. For some of the men, spiritual concerns were either non-existent or thought to be irrelevant. To others it was merely a perfunctory service that simply covered the bases. For others, it was out of raw fear that they came to religious services. Finally, there were a few (for the road is narrow) who were true worshipers of God, representatives of the true church.

This is how it will always be in the world. Christians will be a minority in the midst of a mass of unconverted humanity. These different dispositions are no different than what we find in peace time. Yet the truth is that the church is the pillar and support of the truth, making her the center around which history revolves.

3. EXHORT HIM TO LOVE THE CHURCH WHEREVER HE GOES.

These are things I believe a father should communicate to his son about the church as he goes off to make his way in the world:

- Look
- Prioritize
- Love
- Covenant

LOOK: You are part of the Bride of Christ. Always look for her sons and daughters in the same way the apostle Paul sought for them when he sailed into Tyre (Acts 21:1-6). He looked for God's people and found them. They spent a week together and ended their time talking and praying and worshiping together. In Acts 20:1, Paul called for the elders of the Ephesian church from Miletus, a two-day journey. They knelt and wept and prayed, and then parted.

PRIORITIZE: You are part of a global family that should be a high priority for you. Commit yourself to your spiritual brothers and sisters. Jesus was told that His brothers and sisters were waiting outside for Him and He answered, "'Who is My mother and who are My brothers?' And He stretched out His hand toward His disciples and said, 'Here are My mother and My brothers! For whoever does the will of My Father in heaven is My brother and sister and mother'" (Matthew 12:47-50).

Wherever you go, make the church and relationships with God's people your priority. Make a lifelong commitment to pouring out your love and energy for the church. Pattern your life around the apostle Paul who "poured himself out as a drink offering."

LOVE: The church is imperfect, yet worthy of our love because Christ has made her worthy. We are charged to follow His example of commitment to her and to obey His command to feed His sheep. In spite of her imperfections, Christ still calls the church his "Bride."

COVENANT: Make a covenant with a local church. This means you make it your pattern to stand with the members of the visible church wherever you are. Two are better than one. Stand together whether you are on the battlefied or here at home in your community. Whenever you move to a new community, make it your aim to be a major part of a local church. Find a church and be devoted to her members in brotherly love and service. Don't make a half-hearted relationship with her. Devote yourself to a life of faithful service to the church by engaging the energies of your life for her prosperity.

Here is a sample church covenant that expresses the things I believe we should prepare our sons to fulfill. This is the membership covenant of the church of which I am a part:

Having been led, as we believe, by the Spirit of God, to repent, believe, and receive the Lord Jesus Christ as our Savior, and profess our allegiance to Him, having been baptized in the name of the Father and of the Son and of the Holy Spirit, we do now, in the presence of God, angels, and this assembly, most solemnly and joyfully enter into covenant with one another as one body in Christ. Acts 2:38, Mark 9:23, John 11:26 Heb.11:6, John 1:12-13, I Pet. 2:6, Matt. 28:19-20, Romans 8:1

We will work and pray for the unity of the Spirit in the bond of peace and by the aid of the Holy Spirit, to walk together in Christian love. 1 Cor 13:1-13, Eph. 4:1-6, John

We will seek the salvation of our kindred, acquaintances, and strangers who have not repented for saving faith in Christ; to be in prayer for the spiritual awakening of the lost in our community, and to be a faithful witness of the gospel both here and to the remotest part of the earth. Matt. 28:19, Luke 24:44-48, Acts 1:3-8. Gen 12:3

We will strive for the advancement of this Church in knowledge, holiness, and comfort; to promote its prosperity and spirituality; to sustain its worship, ordinances, discipline, and doctrines; and to submit to its leaders as they are faithful to Christ. Heb. 10:24-25, Heb. 13:17, 1 Thess4:12

We will contribute cheerfully and regularly to the support of the ministry, the expenses of the Church, the relief of the poor, and the spread of the Gospel through all nations. 1 Cor. 9:1-27, Prov. 15:15, Job 34:19, Matt. 5:3, Mark 10:21, Luke 4:18

We will not forsake the assembling of ourselves together, nor neglect to pray for ourselves and others; nor avoid the meetings of the church established by the elders. Heb. 10:25, Heb. 5:5, Acts 2:42-47

We will also maintain family and private devotions; to educate our children in the Christian faith and demonstrate the love of Christ in all of our household relationships. Eph. 6:1-4, Psalm 78, Deut. 6:1-9

We will watch over one another in brotherly love; to remember one another in prayer; to aid one another in sickness and distress; to walk circumspectly in the world; to be just in our dealings, faithful in our engagements, and exemplary in our deportment. Matt 19:15-20, Col. 2:9-10, Eph. 5:1-2, Eph. 6:18

We will strive to avoid all scriptural prohibitions, such as tattling, backbiting, and unrighteous anger; to seek God's help in abstaining from abuse of drugs, food, drink, illicit material, and practices which bring harm to the body or jeopardize our own or another's faith. Psalm 1:1-6, Eph. 5:3-12, Col: 3:1-17, 2 Cor. 12:20, Rom. 1:30, Lev. 19:16, Eccl. 10:11

We will cultivate Christian sympathy in feeling and courtesy in speech; to refrain from speaking evil of one another; to be slow to take offense; to think the best of one another; and always ready for biblical reconciliation and mindful of the rules of our Savior to secure it without delay so far as it depends upon us. Psalm 19:14, Psalm 34:13-14, Eph. 4:29, 1 Peter 3:8-12, Matt 5:21-26, Titus 3:10, Prov. 26:20-26

We will, if necessary, to submit to biblically defined and regulated church discipline for the purpose of reconciliation with God and man. Matt. 18:15:20, Heb. 12:11, 1 Cor. 5:1-13, 1 John 2:19, 1 Tim. 1:20, 2 Cor. 2:1-11, Luke 17:4

We will, when we move from this place, if possible, unite with a church where we can carry out the spirit of this covenant.

How do you help a boy love the church?

First, you as a father must love her yourself. If you take her lightly, then your son will follow suit.

Second, you must take him to church, not send him. Take him, walk beside him, coach him to love the church with his time and resources.

Third, never lose faith in God's ability to glorify Himself through the church. No church is perfect, and yet, still He glorifies Himself through her imperfect members and ministries.

Fourth, never gossip about the members of the church or unrighteously criticize her leaders.

Fifth, don't separate yourself from the church and don't pretend that having church alone with your family is a legitimate expression of the church.

If a boy would be tempted to take the church lightly, and make her a sideline in his life, he should remember that Christ purchased the church "with His own blood," and that she is a "Bride." Christ loved the church to the end, and He has done so in order that we would follow His example to be devoted to her in brotherly love all the days of our lives until He comes again.

"Son, Never Neglect the Local Church"

Journey to Honor My Father

This book is the result of a journey to give glory to God by honoring my father. Some years ago, I started asking my father questions about his life, and every answer increased my hunger for more. So I sent my daughter, Kelly, to be with him, to interview him, and get his stories recorded for his great-grandchildren.

When I was a boy, my father would tell me only a very few brief stories about his time in World War II, but that would be enough to get me started thinking about that mythical island—Iwo Jima. Back then he wouldn't say much, but I still heard about foxholes, Mount Suribachi, P51 Mustangs, explosions, and flamethrowers.

That has all changed. Now he shares freely, and just when we start thinking we have heard it all, he tells another story we have never heard before.

Now that I am older, I understand how powerful a father's stories are. They have had a surprising effect on every member of my family. Those stories have spread out and affected the community in which I live, and they have even spread around the world.

My daughter Kelly's devotion to the spiritual legacy of our household led her to chronicle the stories of my father's life in order to identify the key evidences of the providence of God in our family history. She wanted to leave a legacy of honor toward God for all He had done through the stories of His kindness toward our family. The result was three years of research and then a twenty thousand mile trip from North Carolina to Iwo Jima with Vision Forum's Doug Phillips and Geoff Botkin's film crew, my father and me, and my son David. After that, she completed writing her book about her grandfather entitled, <u>Coming In on a Wing and a Prayer</u>.

A GENERATION PASSING FROM THE SCENE

When I realized that the men of the World War II generation were passing away, I determined to take steps to honor them before they had completely passed from the scene. One of the steps I took was to hold a Memorial Day celebration on our farm. I invited veterans from the community who would come and share their stories of the providence of God to whomever would listen. That annual Memorial Day picnic now draws hundreds of people who want to hear the stories. I wanted to cast a vision for children honoring their parents, and for fathers telling their stories to the next generation.

Doug Phillips, who has been a regular part of the Memorial Day program, and a tremendous inspiration for sons honoring their fathers, has stated it this way:

> God has given us a unique opportunity not only to train fellow believers to better honor their fathers, and fathers to better disciple their sons, but also to touch the hearts of the unbelieving world with a creative, but uncompromising Gospel message of hope to the nation that will honor the Lord, and thus secure their own providential protection, by embracing the spirit of the Fifth Commandment.

> God has promised that 'it will be well with us' and we will 'live long in the land that the Lord gives to us' if we honor our fathers. In my mind, this 'first command with promise' is the single best antidote to terrorism, foreign attacks, and division from within. A nation that rightly honors fathers, honors God."

Exodus 20:12 makes it clear that God's covenantal promise is extended to individuals and nations which honor their fathers. When we honor our fathers "it is well" with us and we "will live long in the land."

Throughout Scripture, God communicates a methodology for sons honoring their fathers.

Deuteronomy 32:7 reveals that God commands sons to interview their fathers.

Remember the days of old. Consider the years of many generations. Ask your father and he will show you, the elders and they will tell you.

Job 8:15 issues a warning that one generation must actively seek the wisdom of the past generation or be judged:

> For inquire I pray thee of the former age and prepare thyself to the search of their fathers; (We are but of yesterday and nothing because our days upon the earth are a shadow); shall they not teach thee and tell thee, and utter words out of their heart? Can the rush grow up without mire? Can the flag grow without water? Whilst it is yet in his greenness, and not cut down, it withereth before any other herb. So are the paths of all that forget God."

Sons have a duty to search after the truth by inquiring of their fathers. Scripture requires it. The lessons of our fathers help us to define manhood, they help us to grow up to go further than our own fathers did. These lessons give us context, meaning, and direction.

If sons do not search for the lessons of their fathers, they will suffer a loss of roots and will more easily wither. But, when God touches the hearts of fathers, He can establish a spiritual dynasty that tends to prepare a people for multi-generational victory.

Scripture is filled with admonitions and examples of this.

In Psalm 78, the Lord challenges fathers to teach the next four generations of the mighty Name of God so that their sons will be strong in the land.

In Psalm 71:17-18, God appeals to the call of the Lord upon the hearts of Fathers.

In Psalm 44:1-7, God speaks of the confidence and comfort sons receive from learning of God's providence from their fathers.

Micah 4:6 clarifies the importance of the unity of fathers and sons that creates a people prepared for the Lord. It makes clear that the absence of this unity opens the door for the judgment of God.

As the World War II generation fades away, we have a tremendous opportunity (and obligation) to honor the men who lived in that era.

Doug Phillips states that "the loss of the stories is not only a national loss, but it is also a personal loss and family loss. Ultimately, it is a loss for humanity to forget the mighty deeds of God."

The Bible makes it clear that If sons do not honor their fathers, it will not go well with them (Ephesians 6:1-4).

In each generation, we have an opportunity to rise up and give honor. I hope this book will be an encouragement to take on this important responsibility.

> We have heard with our ears, O God, Our fathers have told us, the deeds You did in their days, in days of old: You drove out the nations with Your hand, but them You planted; You afflicted the peoples, and cast them out. For they did not gain possession of the land by their own sword, nor did their own arm save them; but it was Your right hand, Your arm, and the light of Your countenance, because You favored them. You are my King, O God; command victories for Jacob. Through You we will push down our enemies; through Your name we will trample those who rise up against us. For I will not trust in my bow, nor shall my sword save me. But You have saved us from our enemies, and have put to shame those who hated us. In God we boast all day long, and praise Your name forever. Selah. (Psalm 44:1-7)

EPILOGUE:

Last Chance to Honor

There is such a thing as missing an opportunity. There are two kinds of missed opportunities. The first is the kind that still holds out a chance to recover. The second is a complete loss of the opportunity and it will never return again. The loss is final and time does not wait for us to wake up and do the right thing.

History is charging on and the World War II generation is quickly slipping away into history itself.

Now is the time to rise up and honor those men. It is the duty of our generation to honor the legacy of our fathers. Some opportunities slip away forever if not captured with a sense of urgency. This sense of urgency has been growing in me for quite some time. When it started a few years ago, I was stunned to learn that about one thousand World War II veterans were dying each day, now in 2006, the number has nearly doubled. In only a few years, they will all be gone.

Missed opportunity is something I am aware of in my own life. We all know the feeling. You get this sense that you need to go see someone or write that letter or go to the hospital...but life is so busy at the time that it seems impossible to fit one more thing into the week. So you ignore that gnawing undercurrent and keep the course, and you later regret it.

Now is the time to honor the men who died defending our country during the Second World War.

As of 2006, over seventy-five percent of the men who fought in that war have already died, and many of those have a very difficult time getting around. So many important stories lay silent in the graves of the men who never told them. So many men went to their graves without anyone either knowing or acknowledging what they did.

These men saved the planet from the worldwide spread of evil fascist governments, illustrated in Hitler's death camps and the brutal murders of hundreds of thousands of innocent civilians who were in the way of Japanese expansion.

This historical moment is not one that I want to miss. Join me in honoring our fathers who fought in the Second World War.

I have met many men who tell me that they watched the film League of Grateful Sons in a flood of tears of regret for the loss they feel because they did not take the time to get to know their fathers. The stories are lost and they are sorry because it's too late—their fathers are already in the grave.

These men end up saying to those who still have an opportunity, "Sons, ask your fathers! You never know when it will be too late and you will only have regrets to show for your desire."

In the same way that sons only have a limited time opportunity to honor their fathers by asking them about their stories, fathers also have limited time to tell.

Fathers, tell your children. Tell them of the great deeds of God. Explain in detail the ways He has fed you and sustained you and cared for you and taught you all the days of your life. Open Holy Scripture and read it to your sons as a springboard for all the stories you need to tell them.

If he is still alive, go back and ask your own father to tell you his story. Then get busy telling your own children the stories that will prepare them for the battles ahead.

Note from the Author

This book in no way hopes to glorify war. Nations often go to war for the wrong reasons that are contrary to the Word of God. Imperfect men conduct war and they often do things that are despicable. However, there are lessons to be learned from war. It is legitimate to honor those who served. It is right to honor your father and learn from him even though the circumstances were not ideal. Even when imperfect men attempt to constrain evil, there are still heroes who emerge. No matter how unlawful a war might be, there are some obedient soldiers with the glory of God in their hearts and obedience in their minds. My purpose in this book is not to glorify WWII or to pretend that it was something it was not. Rather, I hope to take what happened in my family, and see what we might learn from it, and determine how we might glorify God in our lives as a result of the experience.

Endnotes:

THE BATTLEFIELD OF MY FATHER'S YOUTH

1 Lord Tennyson Alfred. "The Charge of the Light Brigade," 1854.

UNMATCHED BATTLE

1 The U.S. Marines on Iwo Jima, (Nashville, TN: The Battery Press, 1987) Vii.

2 Ibid., 5.

3 James Bradely, Flags of Our Fathers, (New York, New York: Bantam Book, 2000) 8.

4 Bill Ross, Iwo Jima, Legacy of Valor, (New York: First Vintage Books Edition, 1986) 31.

5 The U.S. Marines on Iwo Jima, (Nashville, TN: The Battery Press, 1987) 19. .

6 Col. Joseph H. Alexander, Closing In: Marines in the Seizure of Iwo Jima, 28. Taken from: http://www.ibiblio.net/hyperwar/USMC/USMC-Iwo/index.html.

7 Col. Joseph H. Alexander, Closing In: Marines in the Seizure of Iwo Jima, Taken from: http://www.nps.gov/archive/wapa/indepth/extContent/usmc/pcn-190-003131-00/sec3a.htm.

8 Corporal Hershel "Woody" Williams, "Cpl. HERSHEL W. WILLIAMS Medal of Honor 1945 1/21/3 Iwo Jima." Taken from: http://www.pritzkermilitarylibrary.org/events/2006/files/2006-11-16-hershelWilliams-biography.pdf.

9 HistoryOfWar.org, "Operation Detachment: The Battle for Iwo Jima February – March 1945," taken from: http://www.historyofwar.org/articles/battles_iwojima.html.

10 Patrick Clancey, "Hyper War Foundation," Taken from: http://www.ibiblio.org/hyperwar/PTO/Iwo/index.html.

MOUNT SURIBACHI

1 Col. Joseph H. Alexander, Closing In: Marines in the Seizure of Iwo Jima, 20. Taken from: http://www.ibiblio.net/hyperwar/USMC/USMC-Iwo/index.html.

2 Ibid., 21.

3 Ibid., 20.

4 Tim Challies, "Little Sins," Taken from http://www.challies.com/archives/001998.php.

5 Horaius Bonar, God's Way of Holiness

THE TERRORS OF FLAMETHROWERS

1 Corporal Hershel "Woody" Williams, "Cpl. HERSHEL W. WILLIAMS Medal of Honor 1945 1/21/3 Iwo Jima." Taken from: http://www.pritzkermilitarylibrary.org/events/2006/files/2006-11-16-hershelWilliams-biography.pdf.

2 Col. Joseph H. Alexander, Closing In: Marines in the Seizure of Iwo Jima, 37. Taken from: http://www.ibiblio.net/hyperwar/USMC/USMC-Iwo/index.html.

3 Adapted and condensed from CHRIST BIBLE Pulpit, P.O. Box 5772, Oakland, CA. 94605, U.S.A.

THE P-51D MUSTANG

1 Larry Davis, P-51 Mustang in Action, (Carrollton, Texas: Squadron Publications, Inc. 1081), 2.

2 Ibid., 4.

3 Ibid.

4 Ibid.

5 Ibid.

6 Ibid., 35.

7 John Bunyan, The Pilgrim's Progress, (New York: E.P. Dutton & Co. 1918) 351.

MASSIVE DEPLOYMENT

1 James Bradely, Flags of Our Fathers, (New York, New York: Bantam Book, 2000) 127.

2 Col. Joseph H. Alexander, Closing In: Marines in the Seizure of Iwo Jima, 49. Taken from: http://www.ibiblio.net/hyperwar/USMC/USMC-Iwo/index.html.

HANDLING DIRE STRAITS:

1 Col. Joseph H. Alexander, Closing In: Marines in the Seizure of Iwo Jima, 52. Taken from: http://www.ibiblio.net/hyperwar/USMC/USMC-Iwo/index.html.

2 Taken from: http://www.ditext.com/japan/napalm.html

THE MEAT GRINDER

1 Time Magazine report, 12 March 1945.

2 Taken from http://www.geocities.com/rbackstr2000/aa400227.txt

3 Committee on Veterans' Affairs United States Senate, Medal of Honor Recipients 1863-1978, (Washington: U.S. Government Printing Office, 1979) 583.

4 The U.S. Marines on Iwo Jima, (Nashville, TN: The Battery Press, 1987) 145.

BLACK FRIDAY

1 Department of the Navy, Naval Historical Center, Typhoons and Hurricanes: Pacific Typhoon June 1945 (Washington, D.C.), Taken from: http://www.history.navy.mil/faqs/faq102-5.htm.

2 Proceedings and Debates of the 79th Congress, First Session, Tuesday, 25 Sept. 1945, No. 167.

3 Proceedings and Debates of the 79th Congress.

BOXES FROM HOME

1 Richard Baxter, Directions for Hating Sin, Direct #5, Fire and Ice Sermon Series, <http://www.puritansermons.com/>)

2 John Owen, The Mortification of Sin, 102-103.

THE CHURCH TRIUMPHANT

1 Cornelius Vanderbreggen, Jr., Letters of a Leatherneck, (Netherlands: Reapers' Fellowship Publications, 1948).

2 Ibid., 191.

3 Ibid., 193.

4 Ibid., 197.

Bibliography

Bartley, Lt. Col. Whitman. Iwo Jima: Amphibious Epic. Nashville, Tennessee: The Battery Press, 1954.

Conner, Howard M. The Spearhead, Fifth Marine Division. Washington, D.C.: Infantry Journal Press, 1950.

Costello, John. The Pacific War 1941-1945. New York: Harper Collins, 1981.

Henri, Capt. Raymond. The U.S. Marines on Iwo Jima. Nashville, Tennessee: The Battery Press, 1987.

Hoffman, Major Carl W. Saipan: The Beginning of the End. Nashville, Tennessee: The Battery Press, 1950.

Lambert, John W. The Pineapple Air Force, Pearl Harbor to Tokyo. St Paul, Minnesota: Phalanx Publishing Co., 1990.

Nalty, Bernard C. Wartime in the Pacific. Norman, Oklahoma: University of Oklahoma Press, 1999.

U.S. Government Printing Office. Medal of Honor Recipients 1863-1978. Committee on Veterans' Affairs, U.S. Senate, 1979.